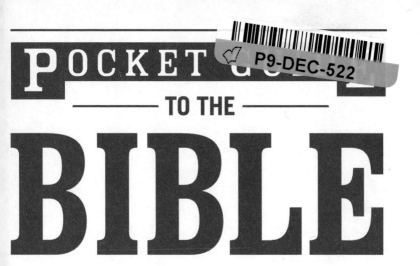

# POCKET GUIDE
## — TO THE —
# BIBLE

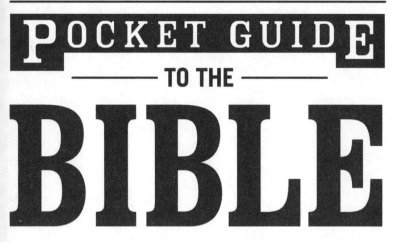

# POCKET GUIDE
## — TO THE —
# BIBLE

## A LITTLE
## BOOK ABOUT
## THE BIG BOOK

[RELEVANTBOOKS]

# JASON BOYETT

Published by RELEVANT Books
A division of RELEVANT Media Group, Inc.

www.relevantbooks.com
www.relevantmediagroup.com

© 2006 RELEVANT Media Group

Design by Relevant Solutions
Cover and interior design by Jeremy Kennedy

RELEVANT Books is a registered trademark of RELEVANT Media Group, Inc., and is
registered in the U.S. Patent and Trademark Office.

For information or bulk orders:
RELEVANT MEDIA GROUP, INC.
100 SOUTH LAKE DESTINY DR., STE 200
ORLANDO, FL 32810
407-660-1411

Library of Congress Control Number: 2005911205
International Standard Book Number: 0-9768175-4-3

For booking information, please visit www.jasonboyett.com.

06 07 08 09 10 8 7 6 5 4 3 2 1

Printed in the United States of America

# CONTENTS

# INTRODUCTION

*I*n the beginning was the Word. At least, that's what some people call it. Others know it as the Good Book, the Holy Scriptures, or the Law and the Prophets. But to most of us? It's the Bible.

The thing came together a couple millennia ago and covers a few thousand years of human history. Readers of the Bible occasionally dispute its authorship. Some people think the book was written by God himself, whispering in the ears of a few dozen holy scribes way back in the Middle East. Others think those who wrote it were decent guys, perhaps more attuned to God than most, who got

> Something like 168,000 new Bibles are sold, given away, or otherwise distributed every day.

the Creator's point across despite subjecting the text to their own personal whims and limitations and primitive perspectives. And some people think the authors were all just a bunch of delusional wack-jobs out to justify their own misguided beliefs.

But don't let the controversy keep you from enjoying the Bible, because there's good stuff in there. Just about everyone can find something to enjoy.

Steadfast believers *love* the Bible, even though right in the middle of it—in Psalms, which a lot of people cite as among their favorite books of the Bible—the authors repeatedly call into question God's faithfulness. And his presence. Even his existence.[1] Nonbelievers and skeptics enjoy the Bible too because this collection of ancient documents packs a variety of literary styles, influential language, and beloved stories about human nature—beneficial material, whether or not they think any of it's true.

> "I believe the Bible is the best gift God has ever given to man. All the good from the Savior of the world is communicated to us through this book."
> —Abraham Lincoln
> (1809–1865)

Uptight moralists adore the Bible despite its explicit references to sex and immorality. Cautious mommies and daddies read this book to their kids, even though parts of it detail some of the most horrific violence in human history. Politicians and judges swear on it, even though they occasionally object to it being displayed in public.

It's a book that has inspired, at various times, the decisions of great leaders of mankind and the obsessions of serial killers. Abolitionists used it to justify their actions. So did slaveholders. It

---

1. Psalm 22:1—"My God, my God, why have you forsaken me? Why are you so far from saving me, so far from the words of my groaning?"

drove Martin Luther King Jr. to push for civil rights while fueling the lynch mobs who opposed him. It has convinced presidents to go to war. It has convinced presidents to embrace peace.

The Bible has motivated its readers to tend the sick, feed the poor, shelter the homeless, educate the uneducated, and fight for the oppressed. It also motivated the Crusades. And the Inquisition. And apartheid.

It gives us joyful holidays like Christmas and Easter. It gives us doomsday prophets and end-of-the-world predictions.

It's stuffed with passages commanding believers to love one another and live in Spirit-led unity. These passages are read by Roman Catholics, Greek Orthodox, Russian Orthodox, Southern Baptists, National Baptists, ELCA Lutherans, Missouri Synod Lutherans, Methodists, Episcopalians, African Methodist Episcopalians, Presbyterians, Charismatics, Pentecostals, Assemblies of God, Nazarenes, Quakers, Churches of Christ, Disciples of Christ, Churches of God in Christ, Bible churches, and a steaming stew of nondenominational congregations.

Jews dig the Bible. At least the first part, which they call the Torah and which Christians call the Old Testament. But Jewish readers aren't so interested in the New Testament, on account of all the Jesus stuff.

Christians dig it, too. They're all about the New Testament, but tend to forget about most of the Old Testament, except for the first few chapters of Genesis and a handful of childhood Sunday school stories.

Yes, the Bible is an interesting book. Which is why nine out of ten American households own at least one copy, according to a 2005 update from the Barna Research Group. It's why six out of ten Americans confess to reading the Bible every once in a while, according to a 2000 Gallup poll. Yet most of us Bible readers don't know Ezra from Esther or Zephaniah from Zechariah. Few of us can list all four Gospels or recite half of the Ten Commandments. A majority of us can't even identify who delivered the Sermon on the Mount.[2]

> The Gideons International distributes more than one million free Bibles every week. Which means people are stealing them from hotel rooms, and the Gideons are cool with that.

That's why you need this book—a handy, easy-to-read, occasionally amusing guide to the Bible and its characters, events, translations, and history. Why? Because the Bible is the all-time best-selling book, one that most people own but apparently don't read, that lots of people read but apparently don't understand, and that people allegedly understand but in a way that makes them jerks.

Let's see what the *Pocket Guide* can do about that.

2. It's Jesus, by the way. These stats from George Gallup Jr., *The Role of the Bible in American Society* (Princeton: The Princeton Religion Research Center, 1990).

# BIBLICABULARY
## (A GLOSSARY OF THE GOOD BOOK)

**S**ure, a lot of Christians act as if a person can just crack the Bible open and suddenly discover "God's plan" for his or her life. But let's be honest, right here at the start: the Bible is not that easy. It's a difficult book. It's stacked with unfamiliar terms, exotic concepts, and complex systems of thought that germinate in the Old Testament and ooze into the New Testament and—hey, what's the difference between the two testaments anyway? And while we're at it, how can you distinguish an epistle from an apostle? The exile from the exodus? A Pharisee from a Sadducee?

How, indeed. Like any collection of sacred documents written in ancient languages over the span of several centuries, the Good Book has a lingo all its own.

For any longtime reader of the Bible—or, perhaps, any longtime

1

churchgoer—Bibletalk is second nature. Every other Sunday sermon gives a shoutout to concepts like sin and salvation. Hymns and prayers call attention to faith, grace, and the cross. Then there are all those sweaty TV types weeping and yelling about the Holy Spirit and asking for your money.

The indoctrinated don't bat an eye at this stuff, but the rest of us? Might as well be listening to ancient Hebrew. To minimize the mystification, the *Pocket Guide* kicks off here with the Biblicabulary, a handy glossary for the scriptural noob. Here are the words you need to know in order to fully enjoy the coming merriment. Strap on your phylacteries, kids, and let's get started.[1]

# ALTAR

Any commemorative structure—could be as rustic as a pile of rocks or as official as a raised platform made of wood and bronze—where **sacrifices** or prayers are offered to a deity. **Old Testament** guys like Noah and Abraham erect altars as memorials for major events or encounters with God. Later, the altar becomes a central part of Jewish worship as the place where priests fire up handpicked animals as sacrificial offerings to God. In the **Tabernacle**, folks see the altar as no less than the connecting point between God and mankind and a symbol of God's presence.

**NOT TO BE CONFUSED WITH:** Your basic modern-day religious altar—the table, inside a church, from which communion is served. It's usually located below the pulpit. Plop a bloody sheep down on one of these, and, best-case scenario, you'll be asked to leave. Worst case? You'll be accused of Satanism.

**BIBLICAL EXAMPLE:** "Then Noah built an altar to the Lord and, taking some of all the clean animals and clean birds, he sacrificed burnt offerings on it" (Gen. 8:20).

1. Don't worry. "Phylacteries" will be defined in a subsequent footnote.

# AMEN

A Hebrew exclamation meaning something along the lines of "I agree" or "so be it." In the Bible, it usually indicates one's acceptance of a **covenant** or is tacked on to the end of a psalm. In modern usage, it's what people say to let God (and any human listeners) know they're finished praying.

***PLEASE USE IT IN A SENTENCE OR THREE:*** *Dear God, if you let me pass this test, I promise I will never make fun of televangelists again. Not even the ones on TBN. In Jesus' name, amen.*

***BIBLICAL EXAMPLE:*** "'Cursed is the man who sleeps with his mother-in-law.' Then all the people shall say, 'Amen!'" (Deut. 27:23).[2]

# ANGEL

A heavenly being in service to God and occasionally interacting with mankind. Angels rescue Lot from Sodom, send out Jesus' birth announcements, bust Peter out of jail, and spend a lot of time worshiping God in heaven.[3]

> In early 2006, a Google search for "Bible" generated 170,000,000 results. "Holy Bible" got 35,300,000 results. "*Pocket Guide to the Bible*" earned an astounding 529 results.

***NOT TO BE CONFUSED WITH:***
Della Reese, Roma Downey, John Travolta, David Boreanaz, or major league ballplayers from Anaheim. Seeing how most angels in the Bible scare the bejudas out of people, they probably aren't the rosy-cheeked, harp-tickling, feather-winged babies we make them out to be.

***BIBLICAL EXAMPLE:*** "That night the angel of the Lord went out and put to death a hundred and eighty-five thousand men in the Assyrian camp" (2 Kings 19:35).

---

2. This is a curse everyone can get behind.
3. Genesis 19:15–17; Luke 1:26–37; Acts 12:6–11; Revelation 5:11–12

# APOSTLE

One of the twelve followers chosen by Jesus to follow him around, who learn from him as he teaches about the kingdom of God. After Jesus' death, the apostles become the leaders of the early Church. Especially once Paul, who receives a dazzling visit from Jesus on the road to Damascus, starts advertising himself as an apostle.

*NOT TO BE CONFUSED WITH:* Aeropostale, a mall-based retailer of casual apparel for teenagers. One sells hoodies. The other wears robes and sandals. It's not hard.

Don't confuse it with **Epistle**, either.

*BIBLICAL EXAMPLE:* "He appointed twelve—designating them apostles—that they might be with him and that he might send them out to preach" (Mark 3:14).

# ARK OF THE COVENANT

A sacred, gold-covered box made of acacia wood. It houses the stone tablets on which God chiseled the Ten Commandments, plus a jar of manna and Aaron's miraculous walking stick. It's kept in the Holy of Holies in the **Tabernacle** and later gets moved to Solomon's **Temple**. Why? Because it's a reminder to the Israelites of God's presence.

*ALSO KNOWN AS:* Ark of the Testimony, Ark of the Agreement, Ark of the Lord

*NOT ALSO KNOWN AS:* The Ark of Noah, which holds a bunch of animals rather than stone tablets and is made of gopher wood instead of acacia wood. Also, it's a boat.

*PLEASE USE IT IN A SENTENCE:* Archeologically inclined Nazis will want to avoid opening the Ark of the Covenant, as it will melt their faces off.[4]

4. This the *Pocket Guide* learned from *Indiana Jones and the Raiders of the Lost Ark*.

**BIBLICAL EXAMPLE:** "Now the people of Beth Shemesh were harvesting their wheat in the valley, and when they looked up and saw the ark, they rejoiced at the sight" (1 Sam. 6:13).

## ATONEMENT

The process of removing or forgiving **sins**, usually through the shedding of **blood** from an animal sacrificed in substitution for humans. After the sacrificial death of **Christ**, the word refers to the restored relationship between God and man.

It works this way: God is holy. People sin. The holiness/sinfulness divide is a significant one. But then Jesus dies as a big-league atoning **sacrifice** in place of humanity, and God offers forgiveness to those who have **faith** in him. The stuff sin screws up? It gets unscrewed. This is pretty much the central idea of Christianity.

**BIBLICAL EXAMPLE:** "He shall burn all the fat on the altar as he burned the fat of the fellowship offering. In this way the priest will make atonement for the man's sin, and he will be forgiven" (Lev. 4:26).

## BLOOD

You know what blood is, so quit acting all uninformed. Biblically speaking, blood becomes one of the most important symbolic concepts of the Jewish and Christian faiths. Blood smeared on the doorframe protects the Israelites during the Passover. Priests sprinkle the blood of a sacrificial animal on the **altar**, and the people of God (in the **Old Testament**, at least) are prohibited from eating blood. The blood of an animal—because it represents life—is the necessary ingredient in the process of **atonement**. Which leads to the **New Testament**, in which people gain atonement for their **sins** through the innocent blood shed by **Christ** on the **cross**.[5]

**PLEASE USE IT IN A SENTENCE OR TWO:** At the Last Supper, Jesus tells the **disciples** that the wine represents his blood. But good Southern Baptists know that, though he says "wine," he really means "grape juice."

**BIBLICAL EXAMPLE:** "The blood will be a sign for you on the houses where you are; and when I see the blood, I will pass over you" (Exod. 12:13).

## BRIDE/BRIDEGROOM

A metaphor throughout the Bible in which the relationship between God and his people is compared to the bond between a husband and wife, a bridegroom and his bride. In the **Old Testament**, Hosea lives out the illustration with the prostitute Gomer, his unfaithful skeeze-bride and an all-too-willing object lesson. But the idea doesn't really come of age until Paul spins it in the **New Testament**.

**NOT TO BE CONFUSED WITH:** All the explicit sexual imagery in Song of Solomon. For years, prim and proper believers figured the spicy book had to be some sort of deeply symbolic bride/bridegroom code. But now, most scholars just think it's erotic poetry.

**BIBLICAL EXAMPLE:** "I saw the Holy City, the new Jerusalem, coming down out of heaven from God, prepared as a bride beautifully dressed for her husband" (Rev. 21:2).

## CANAAN

See **Promised Land**.

## CHRIST

The official title for Jesus, and not, as some believe, Jesus' last name. *Christ* is the **New Testament** (Greek) equivalent of the **Old Testament** (Hebrew) term *Messiah*. It specifically refers to Jesus' role in restoring the broken relationship between God and man.

***NOT TO BE CONFUSED WITH:*** Jesus. *Jesus* is the name Mary and Joseph give the child at his **circumcision**, because when an angel appears to you with a pre-selected baby name, you follow that lead. *Jesus* is the name. *Christ* is his title. They're not interchangeable.

***BIBLICAL EXAMPLE:*** "'But what about you?' he asked. 'Who do you say I am?' Peter answered, 'You are the Christ'" (Mark 8:29).

## CIRCUMCISION

Let's say you're a boy, born to a nice Jewish family around three thousand years ago. You're stumbling around in the hot, dusty desert. Your mom and dad are cranky because the only thing to eat is manna, and they've been lost for forty years. You're just getting used to this outside-the-womb thing—the pooping, sleeping, and whatnot—until you hit the eighth day of your life, and some old bearded dude with a craggy flint knife starts poking around your tallywacker. And—hey! *Ow! There is SO not supposed to be blood down there!* But despite the unbearable drama, you're not too upset about the sudden violent loss of your foreskin. For one thing, it's only a useless flap of flesh, right? And for another thing, this physical disfigurement sets you apart from your archrivals, the Assyrians and Amalekites and Philistines. When one of them gets an eyeful of your scarred-up

> At least ten different abbeys, churches, and/or cities throughout history have laid claim to possessing the Holy Prepuce. That's right: the divine foreskin of Jesus.

penis, they'll see evidence of God's **covenant** with you and your people! Or something like that.

***PLEASE USE IT IN A SENTENCE:*** Back in biblical times, only those males who had experienced circumcision could participate in public worship, which begs the question: who enforced this rule, and how?

***BIBLICAL EXAMPLE:*** "You are to undergo circumcision, and it will be the sign of the covenant between me and you" (Gen. 17:11).

## COVENANT

Biblically, the agreement between God and humanity to restore their sin-tainted relationship. God promises to bless and protect **Israel** as long as they follow a detailed assortment of holiness codes and regulations. And it's a long, serious list. Good thing the sacrificial death of Jesus in the **New Testament** sets aside the old, rules-based agreement, promising **salvation** by **faith** in **Christ**.

> Another blessed foreskin factoid: In the fourteenth century, Saint Catherine of Siena had a famous vision in which Jesus placed his amputated foreskin on her finger as a wedding ring.

By the way, ancient covenants usually get formalized by an elaborately gross ritual. The covenanters slice an animal lengthwise and set the two slices opposite each other, separated by a narrow gap.[6] To enact the covenant, the two parties walk between the bloody, steaming slabs of meat. Symbolically, this reminds them that, should they break the covenant, they'll be cut in half. Lengthwise.

***NOT TO BE CONFUSED WITH:*** A coven, which is a gathering of witches. Witches aren't usually too concerned with God's rules

---

6. This ritual is described in Genesis 15.

and regulations, although the *Pocket Guide* knows a Goth or two who would really get into the walking-between-two-slices-of-an-animal ritual.

**BIBLICAL EXAMPLE:** "God heard their groaning and he remembered his covenant with Abraham, with Isaac and with Jacob" (Exod. 2:24).

## CROSS, THE

An ancient construction of perpendicular wooden beams for the purpose of criminal torture and execution, which becomes meaningful to believers after Jesus dies on one. Having been flogged to a bloody pulp prior to the crucifixion, victims have their forearms nailed to the horizontal beam. Their feet are then nailed to the vertical beam, allowing enough support to keep the body from collapsing, which ensures several days of suffering before death arrives via suffocation. Crucifixion: not pretty.

**PLEASE USE IT IN A SENTENCE:** 50 Cent's diamond-encrusted platinum cross necklace, while undoubtedly blingy, is about as classy as a rhinestone-studded electric chair swinging from a gold chain.

**BIBLICAL EXAMPLE:** "For the message of the cross is foolishness to those who are perishing, but to us who are being saved it is the power of God" (1 Cor. 1:18).

## DEMON

An evil spirit and minion of Satan. Demons occasionally take up residence in people and influence them in, um, generally negative ways. For instance, backward downstairs spiderwalking. (Though this example, perhaps, owes more to the modern cinema than the biblical narrative.) Anyway, while Jewish religious leaders keep trying to exorcise demons with largely ineffective herbal remedies, Jesus just tells the vile creatures to come out. And they obey. In fact, later in the **New Testament,** the **disciples** only have to mention Jesus' name, and demons scamper away, whimpering and farting brimstone with each fiery step.

*PLEASE USE IT IN A SENTENCE OR TWO:* Your mom's neck tattoo of that fire-breathing demon is wicked awesome. Though, as a Christian, of course, I disapprove.

*BIBLICAL EXAMPLE:* "Jesus rebuked the demon, and it came out of the boy, and he was healed from that moment" (Matt. 17:18).

## DEVIL

See **Satan**. At least, look up the entry for "Satan" in chapter 3. You probably don't want to, you, know, actually *see* him.

## DISCIPLE

A follower of Jesus **Christ**. Also see **Apostle**.

*BIBLICAL EXAMPLE:* "By this all men will know that you are my disciples, if you love one another" (John 13:35).

## EPISTLE

One of the letters in the **New Testament**. The Pauline Epistles are the ones ascribed to the **apostle** Paul and include Romans, 1 & 2 Corinthians, Galatians, Ephesians, Philippians, Colossians, 1 & 2 Thessalonians, 1 & 2 Timothy, Titus, and Philemon. The rest of the letters are called General Epistles and have various authors. With a few exceptions, epistles are meant to be read aloud—for instance, to the members of the church at Philippi.[7]

*NOT TO BE CONFUSED WITH:* Apostle. Which is a person. Apostles can write epistles, but not the other way around.

---

7. The exceptions are Paul's letters to Timothy, Titus, and Philemon. Because these are written to individuals, they probably aren't meant to be shared with a bunch of people. Except, you know, everyone who's ever read the Bible.

**BIBLICAL EXAMPLE:** "I wrote unto you in an epistle not to company with fornicators" (1 Cor. 5:9, KJV).[8]

## ETERNAL LIFE

The unending, joyful existence promised to followers of Jesus, based on the belief that physical death isn't the end of the concert. Thanks to the **salvation** offered through Jesus' death and resurrection, there's still an encore—an everlasting future in heaven. Which, hopefully, will be fully stocked with amusing diversions. Because eternity? Is a loooooong time.

*PLEASE USE IT IN A SENTENCE:* While eternal life in the Great Beyond is something to look forward to, perhaps bringing a watch along isn't the best idea.

> "The Bible is a book that has been read more and examined less than any book that ever existed."
> —Thomas Paine
> (1737–1809)

**BIBLICAL EXAMPLE:** "For God so loved the world that he gave his one and only Son, that whoever believes in him shall not perish but have eternal life" (John 3:16).

## EXILE

The seventy-year period around the sixth century BC when the Jewish people are forced to live in Babylon after King Nebuchadnezzar lays siege to Jerusalem, steals its **Temple** treasures, and deports its residents. They don't return until the God-friendly king Cyrus overthrows Babylon and sends the **Jews** back to Jerusalem to rebuild a place of worship. Also known as the *Babylonian captivity,* the exile and return serve as the backdrop for

---

8. KJV = King James Version of the Bible. This is the older translation of the Bible that contains all the old-fashioned language, including not-so-modern words like *epistle* and, yes, *fornicators*. See chapters 6 and 7 for more about the King James.

the books of Ezekiel, Daniel, Ezra, Nehemiah, and Esther.

**NOT TO BE CONFUSED WITH:** The **Exodus**

**BIBLICAL EXAMPLE:** "Jehozadak was deported when the Lord sent Judah and Jerusalem into exile by the hand of Nebuchadnezzar" (1 Chron. 6:15).

# EXODUS

God's deliverance of the Israelites from Egyptian slavery, which they fall into after their forefather Jacob immigrates there during a famine. Having promised them the fertile land of **Canaan**, God sends a former Egyptian and mush-mouthed shepherd named Moses to deliver them. A few plagues later, they're off and running. Forty *years* later, they finally enter the **Promised Land**. It's a long story.

**NOT TO BE CONFUSED WITH:** The Babylonian **Exile**

**BIBLICAL EXAMPLE:** Read all about the exodus in the book of, well, Exodus. And also Leviticus, Numbers, and Deuteronomy.

# FAITH

From a human standpoint, a belief in and reliance on God. It's the intellectual and/or emotional acceptance that God exists, apart from any measurable scientific evidence. According to the Bible, it is only through faith in **Christ**, and his **atonement** for the **sins** of humanity on the **cross**, that believers are made righteous. And, according to James 2:14, the best evidence of true faith is a life punctuated by good works. So get crackin'.

**NOT TO BE CONFUSED WITH:** George Michael's chart-topping 1987 debut album and hit single of the same name. Because, sure, he talks about how important it is to have "faith-*uh*faith-*uh*faithUH," but then there's also that part about how nice it would be to "touch your body." And we're guessing that's probably *not* a **bride**-of-Christ metaphor.

***BIBLICAL EXAMPLE:*** "For it is by grace you have been saved, through faith—and this not from yourselves, it is the gift of God" (Eph. 2:8).

## FLESH

The natural naughtiness of humanity, and one of Paul's favorite metaphors. Most references to the flesh are negative, implying the standard disconnect between human nature and godly influence. Often mentioned in contrast with the spirit.

***PLEASE USE IT IN A SENTENCE:*** When Angelina Jolie showed up with her newly adopted AIDS orphan, my spirit empathized with her concern for the hurting children of the world, but my flesh kept staring at her bazongas.

***BIBLICAL EXAMPLE:*** "For it is we who ... glory in Christ Jesus, and who put no confidence in the flesh" (Phil. 3:3).

## FORNICATION

A good old King James word referring to any sort of voluntary sexual activity outside the confines of marriage. This includes premarital nooky, adultery, and any other illicit sexual behaviors which may or may not have come to national attention during the Clinton administration.

***PLEASE USE IT IN A SENTENCE:*** Just because we did it in the back seat of her Stratus doesn't mean it was fornication, does it?

***BIBLICAL EXAMPLE:*** "For this is the will of God, even your sanctification, that ye should abstain from fornication" (1 Thess. 4:3, KJV).

## GOSPEL

A modernized old Anglo-Saxon word (*god-spell*), which means "good tidings." In reference to the Bible, it means "good news." So, what's the good news? According to Paul, it's the idea that God has come up with a plan for **salvation**, freeing us from the need to submit to all the rules and sacrificial regulations of the old-school **Law**. The plan? Jesus **Christ**. Which is why the first four books of the **New Testament**, Matthew, Mark, Luke, and John—all focusing on the life and teachings of Christ—are collectively known as the Gospels. Also because "the Good Newses" doesn't really roll off the tongue.

*NOT TO BE CONFUSED WITH:* Gospel music, the genre of sacred folk music associated with African American Protestant churches. Much of gospel music dates back to the a cappella call-and-response days of slavery. And though it definitely has roots in the "good news" about Jesus, you'll be disappointed if you head into the book of Matthew looking for Mahalia Jackson to show up with a clapping, swaying, stomping choir.

*BIBLICAL EXAMPLE:* "So they set out and went from village to village, preaching the gospel and healing people everywhere" (Luke 9:6).

## GRACE

The undeserved **salvation** from original **sin**, granted to humanity by God through **Christ**'s sacrificial death and resurrection. Grace is winning the lottery with a ticket you found on the street—it supplies forgiveness, kindness, and mercy to sinners but can't be earned. It's free. Though the word itself is only used a few times in the Bible, the idea of grace pops up everywhere—from God's initial, unmerited selection of Abraham's descendants to be his "chosen people" to God's use of the **apostle** Paul, a notorious persecutor of Christians, as the Church's first theologian and missionary.

**NOT TO BE CONFUSED WITH:** Grace Jones, the former disco singer, friend of Andy Warhol, *Conan the Destroyer* actress, Bond girl,[9] and longtime freakshow performance artist with a propensity for dressing up in gorilla suits.

Wait! *Paul … Grace … Grace Jones … Gorilla Suit.* Look at that: only four degrees of separation between the apostle Paul and monkey costumes. Awesome.

**BIBLICAL EXAMPLE:** "For sin shall not be your master, because you are not under law, but under grace" (Rom. 6:14).

## HIGH PRIEST

In the **Old Testament**, the fellow with the equally important and scary job of being the **mediator** between God and the people of **Israel**. A lifetime hereditary office—the biblical line of high priests all descend from Aaron—it's something like being Chief Justice of the Supreme Court. If the Chief Justice were required to refrain from contact with dead bodies and frequently had to slaughter livestock. Like regular priests, the high priest performs **sacrifices** but also has the responsibility of performing the rituals on the annual Day of **Atonement**, at which point he alone makes amends for the **sins** of the entire nation.

After the Babylonian **exile**, the high priest becomes more of a prestigious political position. The author of Hebrews ties the concept up in a neat little package by referring to Jesus as the ultimate high priest and the mediator of the new **covenant** between God and humanity.[10]

**PLEASE USE IT IN A SENTENCE OR TWO:** According

---

9. She starred as May Day in 1985's *A View to a Kill*, with Roger Moore.
10. Hebrews 5:5–10

to Leviticus 21:16–23, the high priest cannot be blind, lame, disfigured, crippled, or hunchbacked and may not have festering sores or damaged testicles. Something to keep in mind if you're considering application.

***BIBLICAL EXAMPLE:*** "The high priest, the one among his brothers who has had the anointing oil poured on his head and who has been ordained to wear the priestly garments, must not let his hair become unkempt or tear his clothes" (Lev. 21:10).

## HOLY SPIRIT

The third person of the **Trinity**, along with God the Father and Jesus the Son. It is the Holy Spirit who descends on Jesus at his baptism and leads him into the wilderness temptation. Jesus promises his **disciples** they will be comforted by the presence of the Holy Spirit after he has left them, and the Holy Spirit descends on believers en masse on the day of Pentecost. In his **epistles**, Paul teaches that the Holy Spirit guides and empowers Christians, giving them unique abilities to serve the Church, preach the good news, and interpret the Scriptures.

***PLEASE USE IT IN A SENTENCE:*** The Holy Spirit used to be referred to as the "Holy Ghost," until the cultural meaning of "ghost" changed and the term got too scary.

***BIBLICAL EXAMPLE:*** "But the Counselor, the Holy Spirit, whom the Father will send in my name, will teach you all things and will remind you of everything I have said to you" (John 14:26).

## ISRAEL

See **Jews.**

## JEWS

The descendants of Jacob, the chosen people of God, and the

primary characters of the **Old Testament** and a good chunk of the **New Testament**. In the Bible, the Jewish people are known for their Hebrew language, their adherence to the Torah (the **Law**), their distinctive ritual of **circumcision**, and their on-again, off-again habit of worshiping false gods—even though the true God keeps blessing them, delivering them, and otherwise protecting them from their enemies on a weekly basis.

***ALSO KNOWN AS:*** The Israelites, **Israel**, the children of Israel, and a "stiff-necked people" (Exod. 32:9).

***BIBLICAL EXAMPLE:*** "Is God the God of Jews only? Is he not the God of Gentiles too? Yes, of Gentiles too" (Rom. 3:29).

## LAW, THE

In general terms, the first five books of the Bible, or the **Pentateuch**. In more specific terms, the detailed code of behavior given by God to the people of **Israel** while they camped out around Mount Sinai after leaving Egypt.[11] The Law comes in two major categories. The first is prescriptive, or *apodictic*: "thou shalt" or "thou shalt not," as in the Ten Commandments. The second is *casuistic*: "when a man [does this], he shall [be declared unclean, be bludgeoned with rocks outside the city gates, etc.]."

Contemporary believers generally divide the Law further among moral, civil, and ritual/ceremonial rules. Which means the stuff about not killing your neighbor still holds water today, but no one's

> "Whatever merit there is in anything that I have written is simply due to the fact that when I was a child my mother daily read me a part of the Bible and daily made me learn a part of it by heart."
> —John Ruskin
> (1819–1900)

11. There are actually two main collections of Law. The first is given at Sinai (Exodus 19 through Numbers 10:10). The second comes via Moses' address to the people, recorded in Deuteronomy, toward the end of the whole wilderness escapade.

being executed for, say, picking up sticks on the **Sabbath**.[12]

*ALSO KNOWN AS:* The Torah, Mosaic Law, the Book of the Law, Levitical Law, the Pentateuch

*BIBLICAL EXAMPLE:* "So Moses wrote down this law and gave it to the priests, the sons of Levi, who carried the ark of the covenant of the Lord, and to all the elders of Israel" (Deut. 31:9).

## LORD'S PRAYER, THE

Our modern term for the prayer **Jesus** taught the **apostles**. The best-known version of this model prayer ("Our Father which art in heaven ...") is found in Matthew 6:9–13. A simpler, shorter version appears in Luke 11:2–4.

*PLEASE USE IT IN A SENTENCE:* My seventh-grade basketball coach used to lead us in the Lord's Prayer before games, after which he would start screaming and cussing.

## MEDIATOR

A go-between. In the **Old Testament**, upon delivering the Ten Commandments and other aspects of the **Law**, Moses acts as a mediator between God (who is holy) and the people of **Israel** (who are very much not). Later, the **high priest** performs the same function by offering **sacrifices** and other sacred rituals. The **New Testament** reveals Jesus to be the final mediator between God and mankind.

*PLEASE USE IT IN A SENTENCE:* My lawyer recommended a mediator in that nasty workers' comp dispute, but since Moses wasn't available, we just dropped it.

*BIBLICAL EXAMPLE:* "For there is one God and one mediator between God and men, the man Christ Jesus" (1 Tim. 2:5).

12. Unlike the poor stick-gathering schmo in Numbers 15:32–36.

## MESSIAH

See **Christ**.

## NEW TESTAMENT

One of two major sections of the Bible, originally written in Greek over a period of about one hundred years. The NT begins with the life of **Christ** in the four Gospels and continues through the spread of the early Church in the book of Acts. Paul's **epistles** and a few other letters not written by Paul fill out the rest. It wraps up with the fantastic end-of-the-world imagery of the book of Revelation.

*NOT TO BE CONFUSED WITH:* The **Old Testament**, which is much longer, older, and even more prone to prophetic doomsaying.

## OFFERING

See **Sacrifice**.

## OLD TESTAMENT

The other major section of the Bible, in addition to the **New Testament**. The books of the Old Testament are the original Hebrew Scriptures, probably written over a thousand-year span. The OT kicks off with the story of creation in Genesis, then follows the cyclical rise and fall of the nation of **Israel**—including the age of the patriarchs, the sojourn in Egypt and the **exodus**, the conquest of the **Promised Land**, the period of the judges, the united kingdom, the divided kingdom, the **exile** to Babylon, and finally, the return to Jerusalem. Plus, you've got Psalms, Proverbs, Song of Solomon, and a bunch of books by major and minor **prophets**. The last entry in the OT is Malachi.

***ALSO KNOWN AS:*** The *Tanakh*, which is Judaism's term for what Christians call the Old Testament. It's an acronym of the Hebrew names for its three sections: *Torah* (the Pentateuch), *Nevi'im* (the Prophets), and *Ketuvim* (the Writings).

***NOT TO BE CONFUSED WITH:*** The New Testament

## PARABLE

A story used by Jesus to illustrate a spiritual point, usually involving everyday objects or situations familiar to his listeners.

> **The Bible can be read aloud in about seventy hours, if you have the time.**

Most of his parables reveal information about the kingdom of God. Famous ones include the parable of the good Samaritan, the parable of the prodigal son, the parable of the sheep and the goats, and the parable of the disgraced televangelist.

That last one's made up.

***NOT TO BE CONFUSED WITH:*** Parable Christian Stores, an association of more than two hundred independently owned retail booksellers that will likely refuse to stock this book if the *Pocket Guide* speaks ill of them. God bless the wide selection, personal service, and exceptional value of Parable retailers. And as long as we're on the subject, God bless Wal-Mart, too.

***BIBLICAL EXAMPLE:*** "Jesus spoke all these things to the crowd in parables; he did not say anything to them without using a parable" (Matt. 13:34).

## PENTATEUCH

See **The Law**.

## PHARISEES

The super-devout members of a strict Jewish sect during the two centuries before and after the birth of **Christ**. A mix of political party, philosophical movement, and religious faction, the Pharisees emerge as the primary opponents of Jesus during his ministry. Jesus gets along well with sinners of all stripes, including drunkards and prostitutes, but the outwardly pious Pharisees are gnats in his ear. He labels them a "brood of vipers."[13] They get their phylacteries in a wad because his **disciples** eat with unwashed hands[14] and engage in other questionable activities. But it all works out in the end, as the early Church ends up with a bunch of ex-Pharisees in its pews. Including a guy named Paul.

***NOT TO BE CONFUSED WITH:*** Sadducees, another religious/political party within first-century Judaism. The Sadducees are the party of power, boasting **high priests** and other wealthy aristocrats among their members. While they have a lot of theological differences from the Pharisees—primarily involving how to interpret the Torah—the two groups spend most of the Gospels belting out a nice little two-part harmony about not liking Jesus.

***BIBLICAL EXAMPLE:*** "Woe to you, teachers of the law and Pharisees, you hypocrites! You are like whitewashed tombs, which look beautiful on the outside but on the inside are full of dead men's bones and everything unclean" (Matt. 23:27).

## PROMISED LAND

The territory between the Jordan River and the Mediterranean Sea (part of ancient Palestine) that God promises the Israelites—his chosen people—upon delivering them from Egyptian slavery. It's

13. Matthew 23:33, at which point Jesus tells them they've likely booked a first-class train ride to hell. Smoking section.
14. Mark 7:2. By the way, phylacteries are the small leather cases containing snippets of the Hebrew Scripture, strapped around the foreheads and upper arms of devout Jewish men during prayer. In Matthew 23:5, Jesus accuses the Pharisees of wearing really big phylacteries to draw attention to their piety. Sort of like a codpiece for the hyperspiritual.

where everyone's headed during the **exodus**. Thanks to a few
wrong turns, spiritually speaking, it takes four decades to get there.
Upon arrival, they deal with the local population of squatters (or,
depending on your perspective, residents) by either killing them,
driving them out, or enslaving them. Which is rather inconvenient
for the people of **Canaan**. But for **Israel**? Sweet deal.[15]

*ALSO KNOWN AS:* Canaan, the land flowing with milk and
honey

*BIBLICAL EXAMPLE:* "Look down from heaven, your holy
dwelling place, and bless your people Israel and the land you have
given us as you promised on oath to our forefathers, a land flowing
with milk and honey" (Deut. 26:15).

# PROPHET

A human messenger speaking on behalf of God, for the purpose
of (1) calling God's people to repentance for doing something
wrong, or (2) predicting future calamity or coming judgment
because of all the wrongdoing. Such prophecies make up a sizable
chunk of the **Old Testament**, from Isaiah to Malachi. Other
biblical big-timers like Samuel and Elijah are identified as prophets.

*NOT TO BE CONFUSED WITH:* *False* prophets, seemingly
religious heavyweights who claim to receive visions and messages
and other sorts of instructions from God, but who are pretty much
full of crap. On account of how the stuff God's apparently telling
these guys to do is more or less evil, and that's not how God rolls.
Example A: Jim Jones. Example B: David Koresh.

*BIBLICAL EXAMPLE:* "But the prophet who prophesies
peace will be recognized as one truly sent by the Lord only if his
prediction comes true" (Jer. 28:9).

15. As long as you ignore Canaan's substantial population of giants. See Numbers
13:31–33.

## RABBI

An honorific title usually given to Jewish teachers of the **Law**, but not always restricted to the ordained or formally trained. The **disciples** and others keep addressing Jesus as "rabbi." Jesus, however, doesn't always seem too comfortable with the label. Especially when he pops off on the **Pharisees**, who love to be called "rabbi" out in public.[16] Because in first-century Jewish culture, being a rabbi is like being a rock star.

**NOT TO BE CONFUSED WITH:** Rabbits

**BIBLICAL EXAMPLE:** "Going at once to Jesus, Judas said, 'Greetings, Rabbi!' and kissed him" (Matt. 26:49).

## SABBATH

The seventh day of the Jewish week, established by God when he takes a day of rest after the six days of creation. In the Bible, the Sabbath begins at sunset on Friday evening and lasts until the same time Saturday.

God is serious about this day of rest and goes to great lengths to make sure his people, the Israelites, observe it. There's the fourth of the Ten Commandments, of course, about remembering the Sabbath and keeping it holy. "Keeping it holy" involves a host of strict regulations: No working. No loading stuff onto animals. No preparing or buying food. No fire-building.

And the penalty for breaking the Sabbath? Death. Which is why the **Pharisees** are always getting so distressed about the Saturday-

In 2005, a British publisher produced *The 100-Minute Bible*, which condenses the Good Book into fifty short summaries of 400 words each. That allows you exactly two minutes per summary and zero time for bathroom breaks, so plan ahead.

afternoon healing parties Jesus keeps throwing.

**PLEASE USE IT IN A SENTENCE:** It's too bad all those Bible people got executed for working on the Sabbath, because I really need to vacuum this weekend.

**BIBLICAL EXAMPLE:** "For six days, work is to be done, but the seventh day shall be your holy day, a Sabbath of rest to the Lord. Whoever does any work on it must be put to death" (Exod. 35:2).

# SACRIFICE

The killing of animals (and, occasionally, plants) as an act of worship. Most ancient religions require sacrifices to the gods, and ancient **Israel** is no different. Just two chapters after God creates living plants and animals, Cain and Abel give a few right back to him as a gift. Only more dead than before.[17]

Upon leaving Egypt, sacrifices become the focus of Jewish religious life. In fact, God tells Moses the fire on the **altar** is never to go out. Ever. So priests end up performing these elaborate sacrificial rituals every day on behalf of individuals, tribes, and, at times, the entire Israelite community. There are four main types of sacrificial offerings, each differing in how the animal gets toasted/sliced/eaten/bled out: *burnt offerings* (no eating), *peace offerings* (organs burned, good parts eaten by worshipers), *sin offerings* (flesh eaten by priests or burned outside the city), and *guilt offerings* (fat burned, meat eaten by priests). It's bloody and very complicated.

Very necessary, too. God is pleased by Israel's sacrifices. For one thing, it's a way to give back to him in gratitude. It's also key to the process of **blood atonement**. The life of a creature is in its blood, and according to the Levitical code, the shedding of that blood (as a substitute) atones for the **sins** of the worshiper.[18] We're never really told how or why this removes sin and restores a relationship with

17. Genesis 4:3–5
18. Leviticus 17:11

God. But it does—especially when God serves up a head-snapping plot twist in the **New Testament**. With the death of Jesus on the **cross**, God offers up the biggest blood sacrifice of all time, putting the whole system out of business for good.

**BIBLICAL EXAMPLE:** "Sacrifice a bull each day as a sin offering to make atonement. Purify the altar by making atonement for it, and anoint it to consecrate it" (Exod. 29:36).

## SALVATION

Deliverance from **sin** and its future punishment. The **New Testament** speaks of salvation from at least three perspectives. The first refers to salvation as a past event—a spiritual rescue from sin and death, occurring at the moment of belief in Jesus as the **Christ**.[19] The second implies a process believers experience in the present as they are changed by a restored relationship with God.[20] The third is future salvation from God's wrath (a "Get Out of Hell Free" card) and the ability to participate in the coming eternal kingdom of God (a ticket to heaven).[21]

However you look at it, the big story of the New Testament is that Jesus—the Jewish **Messiah**—offers salvation to *everybody*. **Jews** and non-Jews. Men and women. Moral and immoral. Anyone who believes.

**NOT TO BE CONFUSED WITH:** The Salvation Army. Stuffing a dollar in the Christmas kettle will only save you from the bell-ringing lady's wrath. Not God's.

**BIBLICAL EXAMPLE:** "For God did not appoint us to suffer wrath but to receive salvation through our Lord Jesus Christ" (1 Thess. 5:9).

19. Romans 10:9. This is the kind of salvation generally referred to by those who would say they've been "born again," a phrase taken from John 3:7. Same goes for the common phrase "accept[ing] Jesus as your personal Lord and Savior," though it isn't found anywhere in the Bible.
20. 1 Corinthians 1:18
21. Romans 5:9–10

## SIN

Generally speaking, the inability of human beings—whether through outright refusal or a natural condition—to live according to God's desires. On an individual basis, sin is any thought, action, or word that goes against God and his **Law**. Classical Christian theology holds that sin is universal and pervasive. *Universal*: everyone does it (except Jesus). *Pervasive*: every human activity has the potential to be tainted by sin, from sex to politics to dishwashing—especially if all three are done at the same time. We humans aren't good at much, but we've got sin covered.

According to the Bible, the result of all this sinful lust and evil and selfishness and power-tripping is alienation from God. Which is why God comes up with the whole sacrificial system—then fulfills it through Jesus and his offer of **salvation**—to fix that broken relationship.

***PLEASE USE IT IN A SENTENCE:*** If "conveying a false impression of the truth" is a good definition of *lying*, and lying is a sin, then how do all those preachers justify wearing toupees?

***BIBLICAL EXAMPLE:*** "For all have sinned and fall short of the glory of God" (Rom. 3:23).

## TABERNACLE/TEMPLE

The two structures dedicated to the corporate worship of God by the people of **Israel**, at different stages in their development as a nation. The Tabernacle is a portable tent lugged around the wilderness by the exoduing **Jews**. The Temple is a much less portable building constructed in Jerusalem generations later by Solomon. Each contains a courtyard with plenty of **altar** space for all the **sacrifices** and an intriguing inner sanctum known as the Holy of Holies, where the **Ark of the Covenant** resides and where God himself is said to "dwell" (inasmuch as a deity operating outside of time and space can "dwell" anywhere).

When Nebuchadnezzar crashes Jerusalem's gates right before the **exile**, he loots all the sacred stuff from the Temple and razes it to the ground. The Temple eventually gets rebuilt—only to be destroyed again in the Roman-Jewish war of AD 70. And so the next rebuilding of the Temple, according to apocalyptic interpretations of the book of Daniel, will occur midway through the Great Tribulation. The Antichrist sets up his headquarters there. So heads up, everyone. Keep an eye out for "666" banners.

> In Matthew, Jesus' "cleansing of the temple" occurs right after the Triumphal Entry at the end of his ministry (Matt. 21:12–17). In John, he cleanses the Temple after the wedding in Cana, at the beginning of his ministry (John 2:13–22). Biblical literalists insist this indicates he cleansed the Temple twice.

**NOT TO BE CONFUSED WITH:** Temple University, the famed Philadelphia institution of higher learning. It definitely has a spacious courtyard, but any animal sacrifices occurring there will absolutely not be tolerated.

**BIBLICAL EXAMPLE:** "The craftsmen of Solomon and Hiram and the men of Gebal cut and prepared the timber and stone for the building of the temple" (1 Kings 5:18).

# TRINITY

The threefold entity comprised of God the Father, Jesus **Christ** the Son, and the **Holy Spirit**. This doctrine seeks to explain the biblical passages that suggest the idea. Deuteronomy insists that there is only one God.[22] Yet each of the three divine persons is also

---

22. Deuteronomy 6:4—"Hear, O Israel: The Lord our God, the Lord is one."

POCKET GUIDE TO THE BIBLE

said, at some point in the Bible, to be God.[23] And since they seem
to interact with each other—Jesus prays to God, the Holy Spirit
descends upon Jesus at his baptism, the Spirit intercedes to God on
behalf of believers—there must be some actual distinction between
them, as opposed to a surfacey difference in the way we humans
perceive them. Got it? Riiiiight.

**PLEASE USE IT IN A SENTENCE OR TWO:** *You* use it in a
sentence. The *Pocket Guide*'s still trying to connect the dots here.

**BIBLICAL EXAMPLE:** Very little in terms of specific references
to it. The word "trinity" isn't mentioned in the Bible, though
the doctrine is implicitly understood. It starts to take shape within
Church creeds as early as the second century.

---

23. Several New Testament verses indicate this. In Matthew 28:19, Jesus himself
commands his disciples to baptize converts in "the name of the Father and of the Son
and of the Holy Spirit."

# CAST OF CHARACTERS
## (A TO J)

n the sixth day, according to Genesis, God created human beings in his image. Which, on one hand, is pretty encouraging for us humans. We look in the mirror, and somewhere behind our sleep-deprived eyebags and Botoxed foreheads and zit-creamed complexions are teeny traces of the Almighty. Granted, some of us have more of these traces than others, but there's definitely a difference between the common *homo sapiens* and the common duck.

Then again, the fact that we're made in God's image is often not the most effective PR move the Heavenly Father's ever put together. Because people can be all kinds of awful: ugly, selfish, arrogant, whiny, irritating, violent, crude, and occasionally unpleasant. And those are the people you *love*.

The Bible is the story of the same kinds of people. Some are spiritually attractive. Others are piles of crap dressed in itchy Old Testament garb. And over the next two chapters, we meet them—the famous ones, the infamous ones, and a few you've never heard of—in all their biblical glory.

## AARON

The older brother of Moses and a skilled speaker who hitches a ride on the exodus because Moses gets tongue-tied at the thought of speaking on God's behalf. As well he should. Being the mouthpiece of Moses, Aaron gets to prophesy, inflict plagues on Egypt, co-lead the Israelites out of bondage, and suit up as the nation's very first high priest and mediator. Not bad for a tagalong.

**KEY PASSAGES:** Exodus 4–20, 28–40; Numbers 16–20

**HIGH POINT:** Several. Guarantees Israel's defeat of the Amalekites by helping Moses keep his staff raised over his head (long story). Saves Israel from a Jehovah-initiated plague by standing between the dead and the living and puffing around some incense (longer story). Proud owner of a leaf-sprouting walking stick (weird story). But none of these high points really holds a candle to joining Moses on Mount Sinai for some quality time with the Creator (Exod. 19:24).

**LOW POINT:** Gets pressured into making a golden calf for the Israelites to worship while God and Moses hammer out the Ten Commandments (Exod. 32:1–6). Bites it long before the Israelites enter the Promised Land (Num. 20:22–28).

## ABEDNEGO

One of Daniel's three good friends during the Babylonian exile. Becomes some sort of public official, thanks to Daniel's influence, but is mainly known for exhibiting spectacular flame-retardant qualities when he, Meschach, and Shadrach are heaved into a fiery furnace—their punishment for refusing to bow down to a colossal gold statue set up by King Nebuchadnezzar.

**KEY PASSAGE:** Daniel 1–3

**HIGH POINT:** The whole not-getting-burned-up thing has to rank right up there. Being honored afterward by the king is icing on the cake.

**LOW POINT:** Tossed. Into. A. Furnace. Please try to keep up.

## ABEL

Second son of Adam and Eve. In fact, second son *ever*. Given the task of caring for the First Family's flocks, Abel offers God some choice animal parts as a sacrifice. Meanwhile, his older brother, Cain, presents an offering of "food from the ground," presumably grains or vegetables. When God seems to favor Abel's gift, Cain gets peeved, and little brother becomes the Bible's first murder victim.[1]

> Sheep are mentioned around 750 times in the Bible, and the first profession named in the Old Testament is that of Abel, who was a "keeper of sheep" (Gen. 4:2, KJV).

**KEY PASSAGE:** Genesis 4

**HIGH POINT:** The family dynamics aren't great, but God seems to like him well enough.

**LOW POINT:** Killed by his bro. Probably didn't have many friends.

## ABIMELECH

There are actually three of them, but *Pocket Guide* real estate is precious so they're getting lumped together. Abimelech I is a king of the Philistines who gets it on with Abraham's wife, Sarah—but

---

1. The reason God prefers Abel's offering over Cain's is unclear, but sort of makes sense. Admit it: You'd rather have a steak than, for instance, a bowl of oatmeal. Or celery. Right?

only because Abraham lies to him, passing her off as his sister. Abimelech II is the son of Number One. He almost gets it on with Isaac's wife, Rebekah, for the same reason his dad boinked Sarah. Thankfully, he discovers the ruse just in time. (What is it with these patriarchs pimping out their wives?) Abimelech III is one of Gideon's sons who murders his seventy brothers and earns a reputation as the violent, pillaging type.

**KEY PASSAGES:** Genesis 20 (Abimelech I); Genesis 26 (Abimelech II); Judges 9 (Abimelech III)

**HIGH POINT:** Few, even between the three of them. Number Two settles a dispute with Isaac about wells, so that must have been relatively satisfying.

**LOW POINT:** Number Three gets his skull crushed when, during an attack on the city of Thebez, a female resident drops a millstone on his noggin.[2]

# ABISHAG

A beautiful virgin selected to be King David's nurse in his old age. If by "nurse" you mean a hot young maiden whose primary duty consists of lying next to the king to keep him warm at night. According to published reports, though, the relationship revolves only around comfort. As opposed to nooky.

**KEY PASSAGE:** 1 Kings 1–2

**HIGH POINT:** Gets to be the king's cuddle-buddy without all the sexual anxiety.

**LOW POINT:** David's son, Adonijah, wants to marry her after his father dies, but Solomon interprets this as some sort of grab for the throne and offs the guy. At which point Abishag immediately disappears from the biblical narrative.

---

2. The crushed skull doesn't kill him instantly, though. Abimelech is still coherent enough to worry about being known as the Guy Who Got Brained by Some Girl, so he asks his armor-bearer to finish him off. The armor-bearer shoves a sword into him (Judg. 9:54). Loyalty can be icky.

# ABRAHAM

Father of the Jewish nation and the herdsman through whom God promises to bless all nations with descendants as numerous as the stars. Which sounds great and everything but might be tricky, since Abraham (or Abram, as he's known before God renames him) is old and childless when given this promise. Before long, his equally old wife, Sarah, goes preggers, Isaac pops out, and Abraham becomes a father at the age of one hundred.[3] The Lord regards his faith as an act of righteousness and promises him the land of Canaan as his inheritance. Give that daddy a cigar.

**KEY PASSAGE:** Genesis 11–22

**HIGH POINT:** Is told the following, in person, by God: "I will bless those who bless you, and whoever curses you I will curse; and all peoples on earth will be blessed through you" (Gen. 12:3).

**LOW POINT:** Commanded by God to offer up his long-awaited son, Isaac—a fairly important cog in the whole "descendants like the stars" scenario—as a ritual sacrifice. Which is disturbing enough already. Even more disturbing is Abraham's willingness to carry it through. He and Isaac hike to the spot, build an altar and pile up the wood. Abraham ties up his son and raises the knife to kill him—until God calls a time-out. Wait! Turns out it's just a test of Abraham's faith. A freakin' *mean* test, but a test all the same[4] (Gen. 22).

# ADAM

The first human being, created by God from the dust of the earth. Husband to Eve, whom God fashioned for Adam after extracting one of his ribs. They have a nice setup in the idyllic

3. Technically, he was already a daddy, as he had fathered Ishmael at the age of eighty-six through his Egyptian slave, Hagar. But apparently, that doesn't count. Anyhow, Abe and Ish don't get along too well and end up parting ways (Gen. 21). Keep reading for more about Ishmael.

4. As a father, the *Pocket Guide*'s author gets serious heebie-jeebies from this story and would just as soon not talk about it too much.

Garden of Eden until, at the suggestion of a certain nefarious serpent, they eat from the tree of the knowledge of good and evil. Uh-oh. That's not allowed. Cue the Fall. Sin enters the garden, evil multiplies like a nest of cockroaches, and it's downhill from there.

**KEY PASSAGE:** Genesis 2–5

**HIGH POINT:** The title "First Human Ever" carries a certain cachet.

**LOW POINT:** "First Sinner Ever" isn't nearly as prestigious.

## AHAB

The seventh king of Israel and a wicked Baal-worshiper known for making some really bad decisions. The worst of which is tying the knot with Jezebel, a biblical beeyotch of the first degree.

**KEY PASSAGE:** 1 Kings 16–22

**HIGH POINT:** Meets the great prophet Elijah, who proposes an altar-burning duel between God and the Canaanite fertility deity Baal on Mount Carmel. God (through Elijah, his representative) wins in a rout. Ahab is momentarily impressed with Elijah's God, until Jezebel yanks him back to the Dark Side (1 Kings 18).

**LOW POINT:** Gets an arrow in the gut during a battle and tells his chariot-driver to get out of the combat zone posthaste. But the chauffeur gets stuck in traffic (wars being disorganized and everything), and Ahab bleeds to death. Right there in the chariot. When his efficient colleagues take the bloodstained vehicle to a local pool to hose it down, a pack of dogs show up and lick it clean, blood and all (1 Kings 22). Thus fulfilling a particularly unpleasant prophecy by Elijah.

## ANDREW

A fisherman and the brother of the apostle Peter. An early

follower of John the Baptist who later becomes one of Jesus' twelve disciples. This Andrew knows how to pick 'em.

**KEY PASSAGE:** Mark 3:13–19

**HIGH POINT:** Plays a key role in the miraculous feeding of the five thousand by finding the kid with the loaves and fishes (John 6:8–9).

**LOW POINT:** In later travels, according to the non-canonical[5] *Acts of Andrew*, he offends an official in Philippi by advising the guy's wife to withhold marital favors from him. This advice earns Andrew a trip to the local jail and, later, crucifixion on an X-shaped cross.

## BALAAM

A famed Mesopotamian prophet who gets hired by the king of Moab to curse Israel but ends up blessing Israel instead. Four times. But no one remembers any of this stuff, thanks to the curious incident of the talking donkey.

> "The Bible is no mere book, but a Living Creature, with a power that conquers all that oppose it."
> —Napoleon Bonaparte (1769-1821)

**KEY PASSAGE:** Numbers 22–24

**HIGH POINT:** Balaam's on his way to fulfill the king of Moab's curse-for-hire when an invisible angel of the Lord blocks his way. (God's no fan of this cursing thing.) Balaam's donkey hesitates in front of the sword-wielding angel, and for good reason. But Balaam can't see the heavenly being, so he gets mad and whips the uncooperative beast into submission. Three times. By this point, the donkey's had enough and starts whining to Balaam about the whippage. Yep: Donkey. Talking. Long story short, the donkey explains the reasons for his tentativeness and saves Balaam from the

---

5. *Non-canonical*: a book not appearing in the biblical canon. *Canon*: the books of the Bible accepted as Holy Scripture. Now you know.

wrath of the angel of God (Num. 22:21–35).

**LOW POINT:** The bizarre gab-ass situation doesn't faze Balaam in the least. He talks right back, answers questions, even ends up apologizing for being mean. So he gets into an argument with a beast of burden ... and the donkey wins? Man, that's rough.

## BAPTIST, JOHN THE

Son of the priest Zechariah and his wife, Elizabeth, and one of Jesus' relatives.[6] Like Jesus, John's birth is foretold by an angel and is apparently miraculous (Moms and Pops are old and childless until John shows up). John spends a lot of time "in the wilderness"—no one's sure what that means—before beginning his public ministry. At which point he goes public and starts baptizing people, preaching against the king of Palestine, and talking about the coming Messiah. Because he sports a shirt made out of camel hair and is said to have eaten "locusts and wild honey,"[7] John reminds a lot of people of Elijah. Or a crazy person.

**KEY PASSAGES:** Luke 1, 3; Mark 1:1–11, 6:14–29

**HIGH POINT:** Baptizes Jesus (Luke 3:21). Huh. Chew on that for a while.

**LOW POINT:** Builds such a devoted following around his anti-establishment message that Herod, the king of Palestine, has him arrested. Herod later beheads him because a cute girl requests it at a banquet (Mark 6:25). And who of us wouldn't execute someone at a dinner party if asked nicely enough?

## BARABBAS

A notorious prisoner—the Gospel of Mark pegs him as a murderer—at the time of Jesus' trial, picked by a riled-up crowd to

---

6. Traditionally, John and Jesus are cousins, but the actual biblical text isn't that specific.
7. John's locust-and-honey diet, from Mark 1:6, sounds all eccentric and everything, but it's probably just a mistranslation. Contemporary scholars think it's more likely John was munching on a native snack: the sweet, edible pulp of leguminous carob pods. These taste a little like chocolate and come from an eastern Mediterranean evergreen tree (*Ceratonia siliqua*) sometimes known as—wait for it—the honey locust.

be freed in place of Jesus.

**KEY PASSAGES:** Matthew 27:15–26; Mark 15:6–11

**HIGH POINT:** Freedom, thanks to popular demand.

**LOW POINT:** How'd you like to be the guy the son of God replaces on death row?

## BATHSHEBA

The bathing hottie King David peeps at, beds, and impregnates. Then he has her husband killed. Then they get married, but their son dies. Later, she bears Dave a son named Solomon. Perhaps you've heard of him.

**KEY PASSAGE:** 2 Samuel 11–12

**HIGH POINT:** Gets to marry the king and work her way into Jesus' genealogy ...

**LOW POINT:** ... but only after her privacy's been violated and her hubby whacked.

## CAIN

First son of Adam and Eve. In fact, first son *ever*. First gardener, too. While his younger brother Abel is in charge of watching the family's livestock, Cain gets to tend the vegetables and grains. God seems to like Abel's sacrifice of select animal parts much better than the salad Cain offers up. Jealous of God's favor, Cain then gets all teeth-gnashy and kills Abel out in a field. God curses him with a life of fugitivehood and gardening difficulties.

**KEY PASSAGE:** Genesis 4

**HIGH POINT:** Introduces the phrase "my brother's keeper" to modern English.

**LOW POINT:** Introduces murder to the human race.

## CALEB

One of twelve spies Moses sends out on a recon mission to Canaan. Everyone else is all depressed because the land of milk and honey is occupied by giants and walled cities. Which, you know, makes the conquering more of a challenge. But Caleb's more optimistic—along with Joshua, who goes on to bigger and better things—and his go-get-'em spirit ends up saving his life when God zaps the rest of the naysaying spies with sickness unto death.

> Biblical names have great meaning. Obadiah means "servant of Yahweh." Elijah means "my God is the Lord." Matthew means "the Lord has given." Caleb means "dog."

**KEY PASSAGE:** Numbers 13–14

**HIGH POINT:** When the promised land is divided up, Joshua awards Caleb the city of Hebron (Josh. 14:6–15).

**LOW POINT:** City management is no picnic.

## DANIEL

An Israelite youth exiled to Babylon by King Nebuchadnezzar and educated in the royal palace. Impresses officials there with his ability to interpret dreams. Impresses them further with his ability to survive a sleepover with lions. Becomes the subject of the book of Daniel, notable for its fantastic and weird apocalyptic visions.

**KEY PASSAGE:** The book of Daniel

**HIGH POINT:** Gets promoted to the third highest ruler in the kingdom after interpreting the meaning of some ghostly graffiti tagged on the wall by a disembodied hand. And, yes, that sounds like something that might have happened on an episode of *Scooby-Doo*, but it's right there in Daniel 5. Zoiks!

**LOW POINT:** King Belshazzar dies right after the handwriting scenario, so Darius takes his place as king of Persia. And before long, Darius decrees that, legally, prayers may only be offered to the king. Daniel defies this rule, gets caught having a prayerful conversation with God, and gets tossed into the lions' den (Dan. 6). But everything turns out okay when God muzzles the big cats. Supernaturally speaking.

# DAVID

A lowly shepherd boy who becomes Israel's greatest king, not to mention one of the baddest giant-slaying, Philistine-defeating, psalm-writing, harp-playing, ark-transporting, crazy-dancing, Bathsheba-loving heroes of the Old Testament. A major player in the biblical drama and an ancestor of Jesus, who is occasionally referred to as the "Son of David."

**KEY PASSAGES:** 1 Samuel 16–21; 2 Samuel; 1 Chronicles 11–29

**HIGH POINT:** Lots of them. Most notable—at least, in children's Sunday school classes—is his teenage defeat of the Philistine giant Goliath by plunking him between the eyes with a rock. At which point the meek shepherd boy promptly picks up Goliath's sword and chops off the giant's head, then parades the big, bloody melon all the way to Jerusalem (1 Sam. 17). This part is less prominent in kiddie stories.

**LOW POINT:** As king, leers at Bathsheba and her lovely, um, assets when he spies her bathing on a rooftop. Despite already having several wives at the time—and despite the fact that her husband, Uriah, is away at war as one of David's faithful soldiers— he has her brought to the royal palace for a little royal hanky-panky. When Bathsheba gets pregnant, David deals with this unfortunate turn of events by ordering Uriah to the frontlines of the battle, where Uriah dies. Then David marries Bathsheba. Problem solved. Except for the part where David deals with the negative consequences of his adultery for the rest of his life (2 Sam. 11–12).

# DEBORAH

Prior to Israel being ruled by a king, God empowers a series of judges to temporarily lead the people, settle disputes, and resolve crises. Deborah, a prophetess, is the lone female in the whole crew.

**KEY PASSAGE:** Judges 4–5

**HIGH POINT:** Gives the signal for a ten-thousand-man army to stream down from Mount Tabor, routing a bunch of Canaanite charioteers in an epic battle.

**LOW POINT:** Despite the prominent role she plays in the battle, she's mainly known for the violent song she writes once the fighting's over—the sensibly named "Song of Deborah," recorded in the fifth chapter of Judges and considered to be one of the oldest parts of the Old Testament. Among other victories, it celebrates the Canaanite king Sisera getting a tent peg driven through his head. Sample lyric: "...and with the hammer she smote Sisera, she smote off his head..." (Judg. 5:26, KJV). Catchy wordplay, but this is one hymn you don't hear too often in church.

# DORCAS

A nice Christian lady in Joppa, known for making clothing for the poor, among other good deeds.

**KEY PASSAGE:** Acts 9:36–43

**HIGH POINT:** Dies, which typically isn't a high point, except that Peter comes along and raises her from the dead. Many are subsequently inspired to believe.

**LOW POINT:** Unfortunate name.[8]

8. Perhaps this is why some call her by her Aramaic name, Tabitha (Acts 9:36).

# EHUD

A left-handed Israelite hero who assassinates Eglon, the super-fat king of Moab who holds the Israelites under his chubby thumb.

**KEY PASSAGE:** Judges 3:12–30

**HIGH POINT:** Visits Eglon under the guise of delivering him an annual payment, along with, er, "a secret message from God." Very clever, that Ehud. Eglon falls for it, though, and when the king's bodyguards step away so the message can be delivered, Ehud stabs the fattie with an eighteen-inch-long dagger he's been hiding under his clothes. The Bible records this with exquisitely graphic language: "Even the handle sank in after the blade, which came out his back. Ehud did not pull the sword out, and the fat closed in over it" (Judg. 3:22). Blech.

> Using the New International Version, the forty-third word in the forty-third chapter of Genesis is "man." The forty-third word on page 43 of this book is "message." Both start with the letter *M*. Coincidental?

**LOW POINT:** Delivers Israel from Eglon's rule, but doesn't get mentioned with the other famous judges in the Hebrews 11 list of heroes. Why? Either (a) his deceitful way of gaining access to Eglon is considered unsavory, or (b) no one likes to dwell too much on this story, because of all the fat.

# ELIJAH

An Israelite prophet—probably during the ninth century BC—who scares, intimidates, or otherwise troubles just about everyone in power during his dramatic lifetime. One of the greatest Old Testament prophets and, as a result, the one receiving the most New Testament shoutouts.

**KEY PASSAGES:** 1 Kings 17–21; 2 Kings 1–2

**HIGH POINT:** Doesn't die. No, really—he and his successor, Elisha, are walking and talking along the Jordan River when a fiery chariot (pulled by equally fiery horses) separates the two. A divine whirlwind picks up Elijah and puffs him into the afterlife. Except for his coat, which evidently slips off as a result of all the gustiness. The coat falls to the ground in front of Elisha, who grabs it and continues on his way (2 Kings 2:1–18). Ahhhh ... symbolism.

**LOW POINT:** Mercilessly taunts Ahab and the 450 prophets of Baal during the competition on Mount Carmel. When the false god Baal fails to respond to the prophets' frenzied shouting and dancing, Elijah ramps up the sassy: "Shout louder!" he tells them. "Perhaps he is deep in thought, or busy, or on the can." For real: *on the can.* Most translations replace that last part with "traveling," but scholars believe that's a sanitized Hebrew euphemism for *pooping.* Either way, Elijah delivers some epic smack (1 Kings 18).

# ELISHA

Elijah's assistant and eventual successor as prophet and miracle worker. He's plowing a field when Elijah shows up and symbolically places his mantle on him. Then, showing his new master's flair for dramatic symbolism, Elisha unhooks his oxen from the plow and butchers them to illustrate his commitment to a new life. (Elijah: "Hey! Our names are similar. You should be my protégé." Elisha: "Okay. And I'm not just saying that. Here, let me massacre these domestic animals to prove it.")[9]

**KEY PASSAGES:** 1 Kings 19:19–21; 2 Kings 2–9, 13:14–21

**HIGH POINT:** Right before being tornadoed up to heaven, Elijah offers to grant Elisha a wish. Completely missing the opportunity to ask for limitless wishes (the so-called "Genie's Trap"), Elisha

---

**44**    9. In Elisha's defense, he then barbecued the oxen and shared the food with his neighbors, so it wasn't an *entirely* impractical ox slaughtering.

instead requests a double helping of Elijah's power. Immediately nine hundred prophets of Baal show up for a friendly competition (2 Kings 2:9–12). Not really.

**LOW POINT:** Apparently Elisha suffers from a little male-patterned baldness, and when a group of neighborhood kids tease him about his shiny dome, he commits a minor abuse of his prophetic power. Elisha curses the kids, and boy, does he mean it: a couple of mama bears lumber out of the woods and tear forty-two of the boys to pieces (2 Kings 2:23–25). Jeepers. You know the saying "Mock the bald and get violently mauled"?[10] That's where it comes from.

## ESAU

The (barely) older twin brother of Jacob and son of Isaac and Rebekah. His father's favorite of the twins, Esau starts out with a lot of potential. Also, apparently, a lot of hair.

**KEY PASSAGE:** Genesis 25–27

**HIGH POINT:** Returns home from a hunting trip feeling tired and irritable and hungry. But lo! His brother Jacob sidles up with a crockpot full of delicious stew. So Esau trades Jacob his claim to a birthright—his half of Isaac's significant wealth—for a steaming bowl of goodness (Gen. 25:29–34).

**LOW POINT:** Eventually gets hungry again, but that birthright ain't coming back. Jacob tricks Isaac out of giving Esau his fatherly blessing, too. And a blessing that can be traced back to God's promise to Abraham is a serious loss.

## ESTHER

A Jewish orphan raised in exile by her cousin Mordecai. She's among a group of young maidens chosen to replace Vashti, the banished queen of Xerxes I, king of Persia. When Esther wins a beauty pageant and is crowned queen, she ends up in a position to thwart Haman's plan to annihilate the remaining exiled Jews.

**KEY PASSAGE:** The book of Esther

**HIGH POINT:** Enters the presence of the king without being invited—an act punishable by death—but he thinks she's cute and gives her a free pass. So she informs him of Haman's plot against the Jews. Xerxes, to his credit, orders Haman to be hanged.

**LOW POINT:** Married to a guy who kills people for showing up unannounced.

## EVE

The first woman, created by God from Adam's rib when the poor guy gets lonely. Plays a substantial role in introducing sin to the Garden of Eden. Adam's not blameless in the thing, but it's Eve who gives in to the serpent's "You, too, can be like God!" inspirational shtick.

**KEY PASSAGE:** Genesis 2–3

**HIGH POINT:** Kinda hard to beat being the grandmother of everyone who's ever lived.

**LOW POINT:** Cursed by God to endure painful childbirth, which most women could probably do without. Can the *Pocket Guide* get an "Amen," ladies?

## EZEKIEL

A major Old Testament prophet during the Babylonian exile who combines vivid, apocalyptic doomsaying with weirdly dramatic performance art. Among other odd behaviors, he shaves his head and beard before incinerating a third of the trimmings (Ezek. 5). Also moves out of his house by cutting a hole in the wall and transporting his stuff through it (Ezek. 12:1–16). Both actions symbolize something, uh, profound about Israel.

**KEY PASSAGE:** The book of Ezekiel

**HIGH POINT:** Regarded by many as the "father of Judaism," bridging the gap between pre-exile and post-exile Hebrew thought.

> Almonds and pistachios are the only nuts mentioned in the Bible. Unless you count Ezekiel.

**LOW POINT:** Also regarded by many as a nutjob, thanks to all the ecstatic visions, mood swings, and periods of near-catatonic behavior.

## FORTUNATUS

A messenger who, with a couple of other guys, brings Paul news of the congregation at Corinth.

**KEY PASSAGE:** 1 Corinthians 16:17

**HIGH POINT:** Apparently the only Bible character whose name begins with F.[11]

**LOW POINT:** Hands-down the lamest person in this chapter.

## GABRIEL

One of only two angels to actually be named in the Bible. Mainly assigned messenger duties: he interprets a vision for Daniel (Dan. 8:16–9:27) and announces the imminent arrivals of both John the Baptist and Jesus (Luke 1). He gets lots more attention in the apocryphal books of 1 & 2 Enoch, but since this isn't *Pocket Guide to the Apocryphal Books of 1 & 2 Enoch*, you'll just have to look it up.

**KEY PASSAGES:** The Daniel and Luke ones mentioned above

**HIGH POINT:** Occasionally identified as one of the seven

---

11. Other than Antonius Felix, a cruel, tyrannical ruler who pestered the apostle Paul. But last names don't count.

**47**

trumpet-blowing angels who call down judgment on earth in Revelation 8–9. These judgments include hail mixed with blood, flaming meteors, angelic assassins, and so on. That's power, baby.

**LOW POINT:** You try breaking the news to some teenage virgin that she's gotten herself knocked up, spiritually speaking. *And the baby? He's the Son of God. Okay, have a great pregnancy!*

## GIDEON

A judge commissioned by an angel—under an oak tree, the Bible tells us, in a nice pastoral flourish—to deliver Israel from the Midianites. Which he does, resulting in forty years of peace. Known for putting out a fleece to make sure God's really saying what Gideon *thinks* he's saying (Judg. 6:36–40), and for selecting a three-hundred-man army based on whether or not his men drank doggie-style from a stream (Judg. 7:4–6).

**KEY PASSAGE:** Judges 6–8

**HIGH POINT:** He and his three hundred non-stream-lapping warriors defeat a Midianite army that numbers as "sand on the seashore." They accomplish this feat with a deathly combination of trumpets, torches, smashed clay jars, and shrieking.[12]

**LOW POINT:** Melts down a bunch of gold earrings collected from the defeated Midianites and makes a priestly ephod (a special Hebrew vest-like garment) out of it. Which, of course, the Israelites end up worshiping. Because they'd worship a steaming pile of camel poo if you spilled enough melted gold on it.

## GOD

See **Yahweh**.

## GOLIATH

A Philistine giant, who measures nine foot four, sports 150

---

**48**   12. Between this and Jericho, God just doesn't get enough credit for his creative battle strategies.

pounds of bronze armor and taunts the knock-kneed Israelites until David slingshots him into the afterlife.

**KEY PASSAGE:** 1 Samuel 17

**HIGH POINT:** Has the *cojones* to frighten an entire army for a full forty days before they gather enough courage to answer him.

**LOW POINT:** Getting killed by a barely pubescent shepherd boy with a pocket full of rocks sorta ruins your credibility in the warrior-giant community.

# HAM

Youngest of Noah's three sons.

**KEY PASSAGE:** Genesis 6–9

**HIGH POINT:** Along with his brothers, Shem and Japheth, and their wives, gets a ticket on board the ark.

**LOW POINT:** Named after meat. There's also this: following a post-flood vineyard experiment, Noah gets drunk and passes out, naked, in his tent. Poor Ham walks in on the naughty tableau, and upon seeing Noah's exposed, um, olive branch, decides it's a better idea to report his findings to his brothers than to actually cover Dad up. So Shem and Japheth have to hide their father's modesty with a coat, and Noah gets even by cursing Ham's son, Canaan, to a life of slavery to Shem's family (Gen. 9).[13] Thanks, Gramps. Next time, keep your pants on.

# HEROD THE GREAT

Cruel, powerful, paranoid governor of Galilee at the time of Christ's birth.

**KEY PASSAGE:** Matthew 2:1–18

---

13. This has significant fallout as history progresses. Of the three brothers, the ancient Israelites descend from Shem's side of the family, setting an interesting precedent: Israel's rule over the descendents of Canaan, who pitched their tents in the Promised Land. Even more significant is a dunderheaded idea which develops in the eighteenth and nineteenth centuries—that these descendants of Ham didn't just populate Canaan, but another region as well: Africa. The Children of Ham theory catches on, and before long, this passage becomes the South's biblical justification for slavery, prior to the Civil War.

**HIGH POINT:** Known for a massive building program in and around Samaria, Jerusalem, and Jericho—including reconstruction of the Temple at Jerusalem, which begins in 20 BC.

**LOW POINT:** When the Wise Men show up and tell him about the coming of the infant Messiah (who might end up being a warrior king and therefore a major threat to his job), Herod gets jumpy. So he has his henchmen go out and kill every boy in Bethlehem under the age of two.[14]

## HOSEA

An eighth-century BC prophet we know very little about, other than the fact that he and his wife, Gomer, have a troubled marriage—most of which gets dragged through the Old Testament book of Hosea.

**KEY PASSAGE:** The book of Hosea

**HIGH POINT:** When God starts speaking through Hosea, he instructs the prophet to go find himself "a wife of whoredoms" (Hosea 1:2, KJV).

**LOW POINT:** The adulterous wife Hosea hooks up with is a skanky prostitute who goes through lovers like a greasy knife through Velveeta. Which completely sucks for Hosea's personal life, but kills as a metaphor for Israel's unfaithfulness to God.

## ISAAC

The long-awaited miracle son of Abraham and Sarah, who comes *this close* to becoming a God-imposed child sacrifice in Abraham's famous test of faith.

**KEY PASSAGE:** Genesis 21–27

**HIGH POINT:** It's depressing to cite *not* being killed by your own father as a high point, so the *Pocket Guide*'s going with option B:

14. Not to worry, though. Herod dies soon after, which ends up being an even bigger threat to his job than a baby in a manger.

growing wealthy in the land of Gerar, thanks to abundant flocks, crops, and wells (Gen. 26:12–16).

**LOW POINT:** As an old, blind man, gets tricked into blessing his younger son, Jacob, rather than his older son, Esau. It's a complicated story involving parental favoritism, misidentification, a hearty stew, and goat hair applied to Jacob's hands and neck (the better to approximate the hairy-as-a-sasquatch Esau). The end result is that Isaac gets the shaft, Jacob gets the coveted blessing, Esau goes revengy with rage, and Jacob flees the land of his inheritance.

# ISAIAH

Powerful Old Testament prophet working in and around Jerusalem in the eighth century BC. A contemporary of Amos, Hosea, and Micah. Possibly of noble descent. The author of at least parts of the book of Isaiah.[15]

**KEY PASSAGE:** The book of Isaiah

**HIGH POINT:** Introduces the concept of the Messiah, a great leader anointed by God to bring peace and righteousness to the people of Israel (Isa. 9, 11). Which gains him a lot of New Testament footnotes once Jesus comes along.

**LOW POINT:** Spends three years, at God's command, prophesying stark-naked among the Egyptians to illustrate how the presence of God would leave them feeling pretty shameful (Isa. 20:1–6). Seems like there are easier ways to illustrate the concept without requiring thirty-six months of strip prophecy.

# ISHMAEL

The child of Abraham and Hagar (Sarah's Egyptian slave) and the older half-brother to Isaac. Eventually, a family dispute—you

15. The book of Isaiah is all about the life and ministry of its title character, but there is some dispute as to how much of the document Isaiah actually wrote. It prophesies about events occurring both before and after the exile—a span of 150 years or so—which is why a number of scholars think it was co-written by at least one or two psuedo-Isaiahs. The real Isaiah likely wrote only the first thirty-nine chapters. After that, a major mood shift and a reluctance to use Isaiah's name suggest a combo authorship.

know how stressful it can be when you have a kid by both your wife *and* your wife's slave girl—drives Ishmael and Hagar into the wilderness. God promises Abraham that the descendants of Ishmael, since he's the son of Abraham, will one day become a great nation. And guess what? Islamic tradition claims the prophet Muhammad as one of Ishmael's descendants. Score.

> **According to United Bible Societies, more than 390 million Bibles were distributed around the world in 2004.**

**KEY PASSAGES:** Genesis 16, 21

**HIGH POINT:** Inspires the name of the protagonist of Melville's *Moby-Dick*, which is posthumously awesome. Also, at the age of thirteen, is among the first group of males ever to be circumcised— along with his dad—in a big, fun group ceremony.

**LOW POINT:** At the age of thirteen, among the first group of males ever to be circumcised—along with his dad—in a big, fun group ceremony.

## ISRAEL

See **Jacob**.

## JABEZ

An obscure Old Testament fellow with an audacious prayer life. Jabez is described as being "more honorable than his brethren," but is otherwise inconsequential until outed as a major theological figure by Bruce Wilkinson in the best-selling *The Prayer of Jabez* (Multnomah, 2000).

**KEY PASSAGE:** 1 Chronicles 4:9–10

**HIGH POINT:** Appears out of nowhere to inspire a bestseller.

**LOW POINT:** Gets none of the royalties.

# JACOB

Isaac's son, Abraham's grandson, Esau's twin brother, and a hero of the faith who screws his brother and father in a birthright-for-stew scam. God blesses Jacob, changes his name to Israel ("He who strives with God"), and his twelve sons become the twelve main branches of the nation of Israel's family tree.

**KEY PASSAGE:** Genesis 25–50

**HIGH POINT:** Right before being reunited with his brother Esau, Jacob meets a strange "man" late one night near the Jabbok River. As guys often do when they encounter each other in the dark in the middle of nowhere, Jacob and the mystery man start wrestling each other. Jacob must be fairly good at it, too. By the time the sun comes up and even after the opponent dislocates Jacob's hip, our guy still won't let go. Something's weird about this unidentified wrestler, so Jacob puts him in a half nelson and asks for a blessing. Good idea. Because the Anonymous Avenger? Is God. Jacob gets a new name, a prominent limp, and a heaping helping of holy approval (Gen. 32:22–32).

**LOW POINT:** Falls in love with Rachel, the daughter of Laban, who requests that Jacob work for him for seven years in order to gain her hand in marriage. Jacob serves his time, endures the wedding feast, enjoys a little wedding-night action with his new bride, and wakes up in the morning to discover she's not Rachel, but Rachel's older sister Leah.[16] Who's not nearly as smokin' as Rachel. Jacob finally gets to marry Rachel—but has to work another seven years to earn her (Gen. 29:15–30). Sweet love.

# JEHOVAH

See **Yahweh.**

---

16. Either it's *really* dark in biblical times, or Leah takes that wedding veil thing way seriously.

## JEREMIAH

A major Old Testament prophet whose ministry and pronouncements are recorded in the book of Jeremiah. Appearing in the sixth century BC as a contemporary of prophets like Nahum, Habakkuk, and Ezekiel, he's called by God as a teenager and gains a rep for depressing doom-and-gloom tirades—now known as *jeremiads*, in his honor.

**KEY PASSAGE:** The book of Jeremiah

**HIGH POINT:** According to Christian legend, said to have become a big star in Egypt by praying the region free of a plague of crocodiles and mice. Which, to be honest, seems like the kind of plague that would only happen in a Disney musical.

**LOW POINT:** Nearly gets killed for predicting the destruction of the Temple and prophesying against Jerusalem. But he talks his way out of it with a speech along these lines: "I'm innocent, so kill me, and the whole city pays for it. Thus saith the Lord" (Jer. 26). No doubt.

## JESUS

Savior of all mankind, Son of God, Son of Man, miraculously conceived son of Mary and Joseph. He's pretty much the point of the entire Bible, and identifies himself as the fulfillment of the Law and the Prophets (Matt. 5:17). Begins his public ministry around the age of thirty and fits enough miracle working, revolutionary teaching, and spiritual nose-tweaking within the next three years to get himself crucified. Which, in itself, is the fulfillment of a bunch of prophecies. And the start of something that ends up being pretty big.

**KEY PASSAGES:** The books of Matthew, Mark, Luke, and John

**HIGH POINT:** Take your pick: Turns water to wine at a wedding in Cana. Feeds five thousand men with the contents of some kid's lunchbox. Walks on water. Raises his friend Lazarus from the dead. Is resurrected himself three days after dying on a cross. Ends up as the central figure in a religion that changes the face of the Western world.

**LOW POINT:** The crucifixion oughta cover it.

## JEZEBEL

If wickedness were money, she'd be Bill Gates. A Phoenician princess and the evil wife of Israel's King Ahab, Jezebel is so adept at villainy that her name becomes synonymous for a shameless, scheming woman. She's a major fan of the fertility deity Baal and gets credit for inspiring a whole slew of Baal-worship across Israel. God—and his prophet Elijah—are less than cheerful about this development.

**KEY PASSAGES:** 1 Kings 16–21; 2 Kings 9

**HIGH POINT:** Talks her hubby, Ahab, into building her a temple for Baal-worship in Samaria (1 Kings 16:32).

**LOW POINT:** Eventually killed in graphic fashion by servants of King Jehu, who throw her out of a window. She falls to the ground and then gets trampled by horses, her blood splattering all over the walls of the city. Then her mangled corpse gets finished off by wild dogs, until only her skull, feet, and hands remain (2 Kings 9:35). And that's a detail the *Pocket Guide* could have lived without.

## JOB

An honorable, God-fearing man who remains faithful despite receiving a major thumping from the cosmos. Or, according to some scholars, a folkloric character who represents the harrowing plight of mankind's existence in a fallen world. Take your pick. At any rate, he's the star of the book of Job (along with four nitpicky friends) and goes through a bout of major suffering on God's watch.

**KEY PASSAGE:** The book of Job

**HIGH POINT:** Forever linked with the virtue of patience. Has buddies available to grieve with him. Calls on God to answer his demands and, by golly, God *responds*. Said response is a little scary, though (Job 38–41).

**LOW POINT:** Gets the short straw and ends up the unfortunate subject of a celestial wager between God and Satan. Accordingly, he loses his donkeys, oxen, sheep, camels, servants, sons, daughters, house, and his formerly smooth complexion in a life-wrecking series of unfortunate events. Yet despite it all, he never really loses his faith. Impressive.

# JOHN

One of the original twelve disciples and the traditional author of the Gospel of John, three epistles, and the book of Revelation. Owns the Bible's best nickname as one of the *Boanerges* ("sons of thunder"), along with his brother James. A former fisherman who modestly refers to himself as "the disciple whom Jesus loved" in his Gospel.

**KEY PASSAGES:** John; 1, 2, & 3 John

**HIGH POINT:** Receives a mystical, head-spinningly apocalyptic vision of the End Times during a period of exile on the isle of Patmos. Writes down the outrageous dream before he forgets it, and in doing so, not only blueprints the plot of the best-selling Left Behind series but revives the flatlined acting career of Kirk Cameron.[17]

**LOW POINT:** When a town in Samaria rejects Jesus, the brothers John and James think up an awesome payback scenario: they propose calling down fire from heaven to incinerate the town's

17. Former *Growing Pains* heartthrob and the high-wattage "star" of *Left Behind: The Movie* and its sequels.

good-for-nothing inhabitants. Jesus, to his credit, politely declines
(Luke 9:51–56).

## JONAH

A whiny prophet God appoints to preach to the city of Nineveh.
But Jonah's reluctant to take on the job, so he goes on the run.
From God. God being omniscient and everything, Jonah's getaway
doesn't last long, and the Almighty disciplines him with one of
history's coolest punishments ever.

**KEY PASSAGE:** The book of Jonah

**HIGH POINT:** Finally obeys God and tells the city of Ninevah
to turn from their wicked ways and start being nice and stuff.
Otherwise, they're due a good smitin'. Surprisingly, it works
(Jon. 3).

**LOW POINT:** Jonah's inspiring act of obedience only occurs after
God sends a supersized holy mackerel to gulp up the reluctant
prophet. After three days of squishing around in the fish's gut,
Jonah repents. God gags the fish, and it retches Jonah back onto dry
land (Jon. 1:14–2:10).

## JOSEPH (OF THE OLD TESTAMENT)

Jacob's eleventh son and his first with his beloved Rachel.
Known for rocking a "coat of many colors" supplied by his
dad—not the best choice of outerwear. For one thing, a rainbow
coat is sort of a swishy fashion item for a patriarch. Also, it makes
his brothers insanely jealous. But in the end—after being "killed,"
sold into slavery, wrongly imprisoned, and forced to be a one-man
disaster relief effort during a seven-year drought—everything turns
out okay.

**KEY PASSAGE:** Genesis 37–50

**HIGH POINT:** Despite being sold into slavery by his brothers, he ends up—after a long, convoluted, dream-interpreting story—being placed in charge of all of Egypt, in a position answerable only to Pharaoh. All this by the time he turns thirty. Not too shabby (Gen. 41).

**LOW POINT:** The victim of a nasty plot by his brothers to murder him, until they soften up and decide to go easy on the kid. So they throw him in a well and sell him into slavery. Then they smear goat blood all over his Rainbow Brite robe and tell Dad that the poor guy got trampled to death by ravaging camels. Or something to that effect (Gen. 37). It's mean.

> "In all my perplexities and distresses, the Bible has never failed to give me light and strength."
> —Robert E. Lee
> (1807-1870)

## JOSEPH (OF NAZARETH)

A Bethlehem-born carpenter living in Nazareth, a devout Jew, the husband of Mary, and—no pressure here or anything—the earthly father of Jesus.

**KEY PASSAGE:** Matthew 1:18–2:23

**HIGH POINT:** Learns his betrothed wife is somehow going to give birth to the son of God.

**LOW POINT:** Learns his betrothed wife is somehow going to give birth to the son of God.

## JOSHUA

A former military lieutenant and erstwhile disciple of Moses who, following Moses' death, becomes the leader of the Israelites in their search for the Promised Land. Along with Caleb, he's the only spy sent into Canaan who trusts God enough to give Israel a fighting chance against that region's giants and walled cities. His reward? He gets to lead Israel in their conquest of said giants and walled cities. Um ... thanks?

**KEY PASSAGE:** The book of Joshua

**HIGH POINT:** Puts a major hurt on Jericho using another one of those eccentric battle plans God's always dreaming up. This one involves seven days of marching in a circle (around Jericho's famed outer walls) and, on the seventh day, blowing trumpets and shouting. Real loud. It works, and the walls of Jericho tumble to the ground. Wholesale destruction ensues (Josh. 6).

**LOW POINT:** Gets tricked into entering an alliance with the Gibeonites, who put on their grubby clothes, pretend to have traveled a long distance, and butter Joshua up with their knowledge of his great accomplishments. They conveniently forget to mention that they (1) live nearby, and (2) are probably next on God's list of Indigenous Peoples to Destroy. Joshua rashly agrees to make peace with them. Once he learns of their trickery, he has to keep his word and not kill them. That totally blows. So the Gibeonites end up slaves of God's people—which is marginally better than dead—and apparently everyone's cool with this. Even God (Josh. 9).

## JUDAS ISCARIOT

One of the original twelve disciples and the betrayer of Jesus. According to Dante's *Inferno*, one of the three super-evil sinners condemned to the lowest circle of hell (along with Brutus and Cassius, traitors of Julius Caesar), where his eternal punishment is to have his head perpetually chewed upon in the pointy-toothed mouths of a three-headed Satan. Delicious.

**KEY PASSAGES:** Matthew 26:14–16, 26:47–50; Luke 22:1–6; John 13:21–30

**HIGH POINT:** Gets to be treasurer of the Disciples Club and keeper of the cash-filled cookie jar. Which, unfortunately, he gets in the habit of stealing from.

**LOW POINT:** Accepts a bribe from the chief priests in return for leading them to Jesus. For thirty pieces of silver, Judas leads a posse of Roman soldiers to the Garden of Gethsemane, where Jesus is praying, and snitches on him with a not-so-brotherly kiss to the cheek. To his credit, Judas is overcome with remorse after Christ's death and returns the cash to his evil benefactors, flinging it at them in a guilt-ridden, dramatic flourish. Then he hangs himself (Matt. 27:3–5).[18]

18. At least, he hangs himself in the Matthew suicide reference. Acts 1:18–20 tells a different story. Here, Judas buys a field with his dirty money, then falls down in the same field so hard that his body splits open and his intestines ooze out. The *Pocket Guide* prefers this death sequence, if only for its exquisite goriness.

**03**

# CAST OF CHARACTERS
## (K TO Z)

ow that the interminable collection of *J* names is out of the way, let's keep moving. We've got some biggies coming up. Mary. Moses. Noah. And Og, who actually has a little name (in fact, the shortest in the Bible), but is a really honking big fellow. Anyway, our wholly discriminatory character list continues here with a bang—or, at least, a family-devouring earthquake thingy—as we explore a veritable Who's Who of Bible people. Particularly those whose names fall into the coveted *K* to *Z* range.

## KORAH

A Levite who becomes annoyed with God (and Moses) because these two limit the priesthood to the descendants of Aaron. (As a Levite, Korah gets to carry a few holy things to and from the

Tabernacle, but doesn't get to offer any sacrifices.) So Korah gathers 250 of his best holy-thing-carrying buds and leads an uprising against Moses.

**KEY PASSAGE:** Numbers 16:1–40

**HIGH POINT:** Gets a front-row view of the glory of the Lord as he and his followers hang out near the Tabernacle entrance, waving pitchforks and hand-lettered "Moses Sux" signs.

**LOW POINT:** ... which is followed by the ground opening up and swallowing Korah, his fellow insurgents, their families, and everything they own. Then, to keep things tidy, it closes in upon them. Buried alive by the fissure of God! Take that, Levitical rebel.

# LAZARUS

The brother of Mary and Martha and one of Jesus' good friends. Not to be confused with the poverty-stricken Lazarus whom Jesus mentions in the parable about the rich man who goes to hell (Luke 16:19–30). That's a completely different Lazarus. Probably.

**KEY PASSAGES:** John 11:1–44, 12:1–11

**HIGH POINT:** Gets really sick, and Jesus arrives four days too late. By this time, Laz is already dead and tombed-up in a nearby cave. But here's why it's good to hang with the Son of God: Jesus shows up, sheds a few tears, then tells stone-cold Lazarus to quit pretending. Come on out, Jesus says. And Lazarus, in an extraordinary act of obedience, gets up and does just that. Death? Jesus don't roll that way.

**LOW POINT:** Being a friend of Jesus isn't all resurrections and wine tastings. There are a few drawbacks, too. The fact that Jesus packs his own brand of revolutionary faith—and raises people from the dead—doesn't truck well with the religious authorities. And should you have the fortune of being one of those folks Jesus resurrects? They want *you* dead. Again (John 12:9–11).

# LOT

Nephew of Abraham and a prominent resident of the fair city of Sodom.

**KEY PASSAGES:** Genesis 13, 14:1–16, 19:1–29

**HIGH POINT:** Is spared by God from the hellfire-and-brimstone obliteration levied on the evil cities of Sodom and Gomorrah. He and his two daughters flee to Zoar. His wife flees with them until she gets a bad case of rubbernecking and, despite God's warning, can't fight the urge to look back on all the apocalyptic goings-on. So she peeks ... and turns into a pile of salt (Gen. 19:26). Wow. You can't make this stuff up.

**LOW POINT:** There's no "in sickness or in health, as salt or not as salt" in the wedding vows, so Mrs. Lot turning into the Morton girl has to be a bummer. Also, there's the time right before Sodom's destruction when a mob of angry Sodomites insist that Lot allow them to rape his male houseguests. Lot, ever the bastion of hospitality, turns them down. Instead, he offers his two virgin daughters to the thrusty crowd. Thanks, Dad. Everything works out once Lot and the girls flee Sodom. Fearing family extinction— and lamenting the caves of Zoar as a boy-free zone—the girls conspire to get Lot drunk. Then they take the "daddy's girl" thing a step too far and impregnate themselves with passed-out Pops. So the family line continues on, but eeeeesh. And remember, kids: this is the one *righteous* family in Sodom.

> Salt is mentioned by name thirty-six times in the King James Version of the Bible. Cinnamon is mentioned four times. Coriander appears twice, and garlic only once. Paprika is not mentioned at all.

## MARY MAGDALENE

A woman who contributes financially to Jesus' ministry, has a front-row seat to his crucifixion and burial, and is among those who discover the empty tomb on Easter morning. She's traditionally identified as a "sinful woman" or prostitute, but that's not exactly clear in the Bible. If you're talking Andrew Lloyd Webber musicals, though? Then you've got a case.[1]

**KEY PASSAGES:** Matthew 27:55–56; Luke 8:2, 24:10

**HIGH POINT:** One of the first people to see Jesus post-resurrection, she reports the good news to his grieving disciples (John 20:18).

**LOW POINT:** Described earlier in the Gospels as a woman "from whom seven demons had come out" (Luke 8:2). That can't be comfortable.

## MARY, THE MOTHER OF JESUS

A young woman from Nazareth, betrothed to the carpenter Joseph, who finds out pre-consummation that the stork's on his way with a Very Special Delivery. For Protestants, she's simply a faithful servant of the Lord, uniquely favored and profoundly blessed by God (Luke 1:38). For Catholics, she holds a much more exalted position: the individual through whom God became human—the "mother of God"—and therefore a crucial intercessor to God on behalf of believers.[2]

**KEY PASSAGES:** Matthew 1:18–25; Luke 1:26–45, 2:6–20; John 19:25–27

---

1. Recent pop culture—from Webber's *Jesus Christ Superstar* to Dan Brown's *The Da Vinci Code*—speculates that there was more to the relationship between Jesus and Mary Magdalene than financial support, if you know what the *Pocket Guide's* sayin'. Maybe they were even married! But these folks mainly cite a bunch of speculation and gossip. As opposed to, say, reliable ancient documents. Or, you know, the Bible.

2. The Catholic Church also teaches that Mary wasn't only a virgin upon the conception of Christ, but remained a virgin throughout her life. Other teachings include that she herself was sinless (thanks to a special grace of God) and was also immaculately conceived—i.e., Jesus got his sinless nature from Mom's side of the family. Biblical support for this is sketchy, and the idea generally gives Protestants the willies.

**HIGH POINT:** Nothing really compares to being the mother of Jesus, but there's that time at the wedding in Cana where she prompts her son to lend a hand when the wine runs out. Succumbing to a bit of motherly nagging, Jesus relents and takes his holiness public with the water-into-wine show (John 2:1–11).

**LOW POINT:** In modern times, she's resigned to making disputable appearances on grilled cheese sandwiches and moldy pastries.

## MESHACH

One of the three fiery furnace guys in Daniel 1–3. See **Abednego**.

## METHUSELAH

Noah's grandfather and the son of Enoch. Of all the people who have crazy-long lifespans prior to the Great Flood, Methuselah takes the cake at 969 years. Hopefully, it was a big cake.

**KEY PASSAGE:** Genesis 5:21–27

**HIGH POINT:** One of the way-back ancestors of Jesus.

**LOW POINT:** Old. *Really* old.

## MIRIAM

Sister of Moses and Aaron. When Moses' family floats him down the Nile as a baby in a basket—to keep him from being drowned by a paranoid Pharaoh—it's Miriam who keeps track of him along the way.

**KEY PASSAGES:** Exodus 2:1–8, 15:19–21; Numbers 12:1–15

**HIGH POINT:** Once Pharaoh's daughter discovers Moses in his basket, Miriam pops out of the reeds and conveniently arranges for her mother to become the child's wet nurse (Exod. 2:1–8).

**LOW POINT:** Later, during the exodus, she gets all huffy about Moses' marriage to a Cushite broad and ends up challenging her brother's talking-to-God-all-the-time authority. The Lord gets wind of her whining and blasts her with leprosy (Num. 12:1–15).

## MOSES

Deliverer of the Hebrew people out of Egypt, the first and greatest of the Hebrew prophets, and traditionally the author of the first five books of the Old Testament. Raised in Egypt's royal household after the Pharaoh's daughter finds him in the Nile. As an adult, flees to the Midian desert after braining an Egyptian he sees beating up on a fellow Hebrew. Then this out-of-nowhere burning bush thing happens and a voice from the fiery cactus casts Moses as a Hebrew champion. His role? Speak for God. Unleash plagues. Guide thousands of men, women, and children across the desert and into the Promised Land. No biggie.

Charlton Heston won the part of Moses in the iconic 1956 film *The Ten Commandments* because director Cecil B. DeMille thought he resembled Michelangelo's statue of Moses in Rome.

**KEY PASSAGES:** Exodus, Leviticus, Numbers, Deuteronomy

**HIGH POINTS:** Where to start? Introduces the first catchy catchphrase with "Let my people go." Calls down ten plagues over Egypt in an impressive display of heavenly clout (Exod. 7:8–11:10). While making a getaway from Pharaoh, presides over the parting of the Red Sea, which lets the Hebrew people pass through without even getting their sandals wet (Exod. 14–15).[3] Is personally handed the Ten Commandments, and eventually the entire Torah, by God (Exod. 20). Acts as intercessor, judge, and military leader for the Israelites. Gets played by Charlton Heston in a Cecil B. DeMille epic. But none of that stuff holds a candle to this: "The Lord would speak to Moses face to face, as a man speaks with his friend" (Exod. 33:11). Earn yourself the title "God's Friend," and you're golden.

*LOW POINT:* Delivers the Hebrews out of Egypt, but can't deliver them from their grumbling, dissatisfied, golden-calf-worshiping behavior. As a result, they get condemned to forty years of not asking for directions in the desert, and Moses dies in Moab at the age of 120 before leading them into the Promised Land. He gets to see it, though, from the top of Mount Nebo (Deut. 34:1–4). Nice view, but it's not the same.

# NEBUCHADNEZZAR

King of Babylon from 605–562 BC who puts the hurt on Jerusalem midway through his reign, destroys its Temple, and deports its citizens to Babylon. He's a major military overachiever and gets credit for constructing the famous Hanging Gardens of Babylon, but is primarily known for having bad dreams and throwing three guys into a fireplace.

*KEY PASSAGES:* 2 Kings 24–25; Daniel 2–4

*HIGH POINT:* Pretty successful with all the conquering.

*LOW POINT:* Gets a little too pleased with his personal achievements, so God humbles him with a generous dose of the Crazy. Nebuchadnezzar flees to the wilderness, where he stops cutting his hair and fingernails and ends up eating grass like an ox.

---

3. Many modern scholars categorize "Red Sea" as a mistranslation of the ancient Hebrew, which probably ought to be more accurately translated as "Sea of Reeds." But no one knows what body of water this refers to. Ideas? Maybe the shallow Lake Timsah, north of the Gulf of Suez. Or the marshy, reedy Nile Delta. But neither is quite as impressive as the Red Sea. And it's tough to drown an entire army in, like, six inches of swampwater. (Though you could really mess up their footwear.) Anyway, the mystery remains.

After seven years of learning his lesson, he gets better and returns to his position as king. Call it a sabbatical (Dan. 4).

# NEPHILIM

Mighty mysterious men of old, from before the flood. Described as the unnatural offspring of naughty liaisons between "sons of God" (identity unknown) and hot young human females.

**KEY PASSAGE:** Genesis 6:1–4

**HIGH POINT:** Giant in stature. Sweet military skills.

**LOW POINT:** Not enough room in the ark for a bunch of giants. Sorry, fellas. Hey, look, it's raining![4]

# NOAH

Speaking of the flood, here's the boat driver himself. Father of Shem, Ham, and Japheth, and the builder of the ark, which allows his family and a whole herd of animals to survive God's wrathful deluge. Also credited with planting the first vineyard (admirable!) and becoming the first drunk (less admirable!). But mostly known as the cute bearded guy who wrangles cute hippos and lions and doves while on a cute boat in all the children's cute Bible stories. Which conveniently leave out the part about the *entire rest of the world drowning to death*.

**KEY PASSAGE:** Genesis 5–9

**HIGH POINT:** Apparently the only righteous man around, so God gives him advance warning about the impending doom. Also supplies him with a do-it-yourself ark-building kit. Virtue has its privileges.

**LOW POINT:** Post-flood, drinks himself into a wine-induced coma and passes out with his own personal two-by-twos on prominent display. Which leads to an awkward scenario in which

---

4. But wait! The Hebrew spies in Numbers 13 describe having seen the Nephilim—or at least their descendents—hanging out all giant-like in the Promised Land. Maybe they survived the flood? Or sneaked aboard the ark and hid behind the giraffes? Another mystery.

he has to curse his son, Ham, for getting an eyeful (Gen. 9). Who knew the heroes of the faith had body-image issues?

## OG

The giant king of Bashan who rules over sixty heavily fortified, walled cities. Until the Moses-led Israelites utterly destroy him, his family, his people, and his kingdom in their conquest of Canaan.

**KEY PASSAGES:** Numbers 21:33–35, 32:33; Deuteronomy 3:1–11

**HIGH POINT:** According to the Deuteronomy passage, Og is the proud owner of a tricked-out, giant-sized iron bed, nine cubits long and four cubits wide (thirteen feet by six feet).

**LOW POINT:** Spacious sleeping quarters aren't much use when you're dead.

## ONESIMUS

A slave of Philemon, a Christian in Colossus, who goes on the lam and ends up hanging out with Paul in Rome, where Onesimus becomes a believer.

**KEY PASSAGE:** The book of Philemon

**HIGH POINT:** Inspires a book of the Bible. Paul writes a letter to Philemon, the former owner of Onesimus, kindly offering to cover any lost-slave expenses out of his own pocket.

**LOW POINT:** The compensation is a nice gesture and everything, but then Paul goes and recommends that Philemon accept Onesimus back into his service, not so much as a slave but as a beloved brother. But pretty much still a slave.

## PAUL

A big-time hater of Christians, a rabbinical student of the

influential Gamaliel, and a Pharisee so strict in his beliefs that he takes it upon himself to personally destroy the growing movement of Jesus followers. Until Jesus himself appears to Paul—who, at the time, is going by the name "Saul"—in a blinding light show on the road to Damascus. Saul/Paul gets a heavy injection of faith and becomes Christianity's first and foremost theologian. Also its most famous convert. Other than Stephen Baldwin, of course.

**KEY PASSAGES:** Acts 9, 13–28; Romans; the New Testament from 1 Corinthians through Philemon

**HIGH POINT:** His letters to various churches and individuals end up forming about half of the New Testament. Almost single-handedly spreads Christianity across Asia Minor and Greece by planting and leading churches during his missionary journeys.

**LOW POINT:** The *Pocket Guide* hands the mic over to Paul himself: "Five times I received from the Jews the forty lashes minus one. Three times I was beaten with rods, once I was stoned, three times I was shipwrecked, I spent a night and a day in the open sea … I have been in danger from rivers, in danger from bandits, in danger from my own countrymen, in danger from Gentiles; in danger in the city, in danger in the country, in danger at sea; and in danger from false brothers" (2 Cor. 11:24–26). Also: temporary blindness. Christianity isn't for sissies.

# PETER

A fisherman and the most famous of the original twelve disciples chosen by Jesus. Originally named Simon until Jesus renames him.[5] Known for his first-one-outta-the-boat-walking-on-water faith as well as his dunderheaded brashness (which gets him constantly rebuked by Jesus, who once becomes so riled up he calls Peter "Satan").[6]

---

5. Mark 3:16. "Peter" comes from an Aramaic name that means "Rock"—a pretty kickin' name for a fisherman.
6. Matthew 16:23. Peter had to be less enthused about *this* nickname.

*KEY PASSAGES:* Matthew, Mark, Luke, John, Acts 2–5 &
10–12, 1 & 2 Peter

*HIGH POINT:* Becomes the main leader of the Church in
Jerusalem following Christ's death, resurrection, and ascension.
Plays a central role, along with Paul, in expanding Christianity
from a Jewish sect to a full-fledged religion in just a few decades.
Catholic tradition credits him, later in his life, with becoming the
first bishop of Rome and therefore the first pope.

*LOW POINT:* Famously denies Jesus three times "before the cock
crows" when confronted about their relationship on the night Jesus
is arrested (Matt. 26:69–75). Legendarily crucified upside-down
at the site of Saint Peter's Basilica in Rome. Remains in today's
collective conscience primarily as the guy patrolling the gates of
heaven in corny jokes.

## PONTIUS PILATE

The Roman governor of Judea at the time of Jesus' arrest who
sorta reluctantly gives the thumbs-up for his execution.

*KEY PASSAGES:* Matthew 27; Mark 15; Luke 23; John 18–19

*HIGH POINT:* Presides over the most famous trial in history.
In the biblical account, Pilate's not quite the hardhearted baddie
history portrays him to be. Luke and John both record him telling
the crowd he finds "no basis for a charge against him" (John
18:38).

*LOW POINT:* But it's not like he agonizes at length over the
decision or anything. Just a few verses later, he's bowing to a
massive dose of peer pressure, releasing the criminal Barabbas,
washing his hands of the matter, and sending Jesus off for a
scourging.

# POTIPHAR'S WIFE

Sure, Potiphar is the officer and captain in Pharaoh's guard. It's Potiphar who buys Joseph as a slave from the Ishmaelites. But the most interesting character in the whole story is the guy's unnamed hoochie of a wife, who gets the hots for her handsome new slave and conspires to introduce him to some illicit Egyptian lovin'.

**KEY PASSAGE:** Genesis 39

**HIGH POINT:** When the upright, loyal Joseph rejects her sultry come-hithers—at one point fleeing the house so quickly that she's left holding his coat—Mrs. Potiphar falsely accuses him of rape and gets him shipped off to the slammer.

**LOW POINT:** The subject of a whole chapter in Genesis, but no one thinks to reveal her actual name. Blasted sexist patriarchs!

# RAHAB

A prostitute with prime wall-view real estate in Jericho who offers shelter to the two spies sent by Joshua to scope out the imposing city. She hides the spies, then helps them escape—with one condition: they protect her when Israel overthrows the city. Done.

**KEY PASSAGES:** Joshua 2, 6

**HIGH POINT:** After the walls fall, the Israelites destroy the entire city, except for Rahab and her family. And this Gentile hooker eventually shows up in the genealogy leading up to Jesus (Matt. 1:5).

**LOW POINT:** Not the only Rahab in the Bible, as she shares her name with a mythological chaos monster prominent in Babylonian and Canaanite religions (see Isaiah 51:9). Biblically, this can result in some amusing cases of mistaken identity, because who knew that Jesus had a chaos monster in his ancestry? Freak-ay.

# REBEKAH

Wife of Isaac and mother of Jacob and Esau. Rebekah steps foot in the biblical narrative when Abraham sends his chief servant to Mesopotamia for the main purpose of rounding up a wife for his son. He discovers a nice-looking virgin at a well (Gen. 24:16) who offers to draw water for him and his camels. Truly, she must be a fine wife, the servant thinks, and before long Rebekah and Isaac hook up.

**KEY PASSAGE:** Genesis 24–27

**HIGH POINT:** After twenty years of infertility, finally gives birth to twins. It's a tough pregnancy, because those rascally boys keep shoving each other around in the womb (Gen.25:22–23). This has significant meaning.[7]

**LOW POINT:** Not up for any "Mommy of the Year" awards. Rebekah always favors Jacob, and with a combination of tasty food and hairy goat skin, she helps the kid trick Dad into blessing him rather than poor, hairy Esau (Gen. 27).

# SAMSON

Israel's first superhero and one of the most flamboyant of the Old Testament judges. You know he's going to hit it big when an angel announces his pending arrival (Judg. 13:2–7), informing the kid's future parents that young Samson is to take, from birth, the Nazirite vow—no drinking alcohol, no cutting of hair, and no touching dead bodies. Some people become really holy when they take this vow. But Samson? He gets super strength and turns into a one-man Old Testament killing machine.

**KEY PASSAGE:** Judges 13–16

**HIGH POINT:** Especially skilled at slaughter. Tears a lion apart with his bare hands (Judg. 14:5–9). Kills thirty men after his

---

7. Esau is the ancestor of the Edomites, and Jacob is, of course, the father of the twelve tribes of Israel. The neighboring Edomites and Israelites take potshots at each other throughout much of biblical history.

Philistine wife squeals the answer to a riddle to some wedding guests (Judg. 14:19). Kills a thousand—yep, *thousand*—Philistines with the jawbone of a donkey when they go on the offensive in response to his constant killing sprees (Judg. 15:14–17). Then, blind and humiliated after being imprisoned, thanks to Delilah's treachery, he dies in the act of destroying the temple of Dagon,[8] offing thousands of Philistines in the process (Judg. 16:28–30). Sweet payback.

> Samson gets all the credit for striking down a thousand Philistines with a donkey jawbone. But don't forget about Shamgar. Way before Samson came along, Shamgar killed six hundred Philistines with an oxgoad—a pointy, seven-foot-long stick (Judg. 3:31). Not too shabby.

*LOW POINT:* Delilah. Samson crushes big-time on her, so the Philistines put her on their payroll. Her job: to find out what makes Samson so Philistine-slayingly awesome. Eventually she sweet-talks the secret out of him—turns out his strength comes from his long hair—and lops off the mullet while he's asleep. Samson turns into a regular patsy. The Philistines poke out his eyes and force him into a life of grain-grinding slavery. But then his follicles kick back into gear, and when the hair grows long again, he gets the last laugh.

## SAMUEL

Israel's last judge and first prophet after Moses. He's holy from the get-go and the answer to his mom's longtime prayers. She immediately hands Samuel over to Eli, the chief priest, so the kid can grow up in service to God. After hearing God's voice and building up some prophecy muscle even as a little kid, Samuel ends

8. An ancient Semitic fertility god.

up with a dual role as God's mouthpiece to the nation and its leader until Saul takes the throne.

**KEY PASSAGES:** 1 Samuel 1–3, 7–12

**HIGH POINT:** Under instructions from God, gets to anoint Saul as Israel's first king (1 Sam. 9–10).

**LOW POINT:** Under instructions from God, gets to tell Saul he's been fired as king for ignoring the "obeying God" part of his job description (1 Sam. 15:10–35).

## SATAN

God's adversary—traditionally a fallen angel—who roams the earth tempting, opposing, and otherwise pestering God's people. Other than an introductory role in the book of Job and the big Garden of Eden bombshell, Satan doesn't get much play in the Old Testament. Then Jesus arrives, and the action perks up a bit for the Angel of Darkness.

**KEY PASSAGES:** Genesis 3; Job 1:6–12, 2:1–7; Luke 4:1–13

**HIGH POINT:** Disguised as a serpent, convinces Eve to add fruit to her diet, thus introducing sin to the formerly shiny, happy Garden of Eden (Gen. 3).

**LOW POINT:** Squares off against Jesus in the wilderness and loses. Despite being tempted with ultimate power and glory and other deific niceties, Jesus just quotes a little Scripture at him and hardly seems perturbed. Probably because he knows what's coming later: in Revelation 20:10, Satan gets tossed into the lake of fire, where he will be punished day and night forever and ever and ever. Or longer, if that's what it takes.

## SAUL

The first king of Israel, apparently chosen for any one of three reasons: (1) the prophet Samuel anoints him, in private, and tells him to get ready to lead God's people; (2) Samuel gathers all the people of Israel together, at which point everyone notices that, hey, that Saul dude is a head taller than everyone else (give him a crown!); (3) the armies of Nahash the Ammonite threaten the city of Jahesh, and Saul—by cutting up his oxen and dispatching the pieces throughout Israel in some sort of primitive-but-oddly-effective military recruitment scheme—gathers a serious army to come to their aid. Anyway, after all this stuff happens? Israel gets kinged.

**KEY PASSAGE:** 1 Samuel 9–31

**HIGH POINT:** By becoming king, unites a loose affiliation of autonomous tribes into the nation of Israel. Occasionally acts under the direct influence of the Spirit of God, with undeniable results (including the aforementioned ox-chopping bit, from 1 Samuel 11).

**LOW POINT:** God rejects Saul as king when he muffs it big-time by not following God's directions down to the jot and tittle. God orders Israel to destroy the hated Amalekites—all men, women, children, babies, cattle, sheep, camels, donkeys, and domesticated housepets are to be killed.[9] Period. But Saul, upon defeating the Amalekites in battle, spares their king and keeps the best sheep and cattle to offer as a sacrifice. The Lord is not pleased. In fact, he's kinda sorry he made Saul king in the first place (1 Sam. 15:35). Let that be a lesson to you: if God tells you to kill a bunch of people and their animals, you'd better do it.

# SHADRACH

One of the three fiery furnace guys in Daniel 1–3. See **Abednego**.

---

9. This particularly malicious instruction (from 1 Samuel 15:3) is, according to God, the Amalekites' punishment for generally being a thorn in Israel's flesh, dating all the way back to the Moses-led exodus out of Egypt.

# SIMON THE MAGICIAN

A conjurer, also known as Simon Magus, who earns quite a following in Samaria for his David Blaine–like ability to amaze the locals with first-century levitation stunts. Until the evangelist Philip shows up and tells the Simon-spooked locals about the power of Jesus Christ and the good news of the Gospel, and they all convert.

**KEY PASSAGE:** Acts 8:5–25

**HIGH POINT:** Believes and is baptized along with the rest of the Samaritans, and is an up-close-and-personal witness to some of Philip's miracles.

**LOW POINT:** Peter and John emerge at the Samaritan revival and start laying hands on people and filling them with the power of the Holy Spirit. Simon, in a prominent display of magician's dorkiness, thinks this is *awesome*, so he offers cash to the apostles in exchange for the ability to wield the power of the Spirit. Um, no. Peter is shocked—*shocked!*—and blows up at the guy for wearing his bad intentions on his sleeve. Meanwhile, the English language gets a cool word from the story: *simony*, the sin of putting a price tag on spiritual things.[10]

# SOLOMON

Son of David and Bathsheba and the third king of Israel. Known primarily for being super smart, super rich, super powerful, and super active in bed, thanks to his seven hundred wives, three hundred concubines (1 Kings 11:3), and steamy love poetry (Song of Solomon). Also renowned for building the Temple in Jerusalem, a magnificent construction considered by many to be—hang on, seven hundred wives? Sweet spawning salmon!

**KEY PASSAGES:** 1 Kings 1–11; 2 Chronicles 1–9

**HIGH POINT:** God appears to Solomon in a dream, offers to

---

10. In later, non-canonical writings, Simon gets credit for starting up the Gnostic heresies.

grant him one request, and Solomon *nails* it: he asks for wisdom. God digs the answer and piles wisdom and understanding on him like sand on the seashore. Then God drops a bonus, adding honor and great wealth to the wisdom. Excellent dream score (1 Kings 3:1–15).

**LOW POINT:** That many wives? Guy can't have been *too* freaking smart.

## TIMOTHY

A young Christian befriended by Paul, who becomes the apostle's frequent traveling companion/assistant during his later missionary journeys. Most notably the recipient of two canonical letters, the last of which is the final letter Paul writes before he dies.

**KEY PASSAGES:** Acts 16–18; 1 & 2 Timothy

**HIGH POINT:** Gets to work alongside and learn from the most significant figure of the early Church.

**LOW POINT:** One of the things he learns is that as an uncircumcised Gentile, he probably needs to go under the knife in order to maintain a good witness among the Jews. Because apparently the Jews go around peeking beneath the robes of missionaries … This is unclear, but it's important enough for Paul to personally circumcise Timothy—an adult, mind you—prior to hitting the road (Acts 16:3). And if there's anything that really cements a friendship, it's having your buddy lop off your foreskin.

## URIAH

A Hittite and one of King David's "mighty men," and unfortunately the husband of Bathsheba. You remember her: she engages in a little soapy rooftop bathing, David steals a king-sized peep at her bubbles, and things progress quickly from there. All while Uriah is out attacking the Ammonite city of Rabbah in faithful service to David. And though Bathsheba ends up pregnant, Uriah's the one who gets royally screwed.

**KEY PASSAGE:** 2 Samuel 11

**HIGH POINT:** Trying to cover up Bathsheba's knocked-upness, David brings Uriah home early from the war to, hopefully, get him a little non-battlefield action. But Uriah's such a goodhearted, faithful soldier—why does he deserve a mid-war vacation in the arms of his wife when the rest of the guys are sleeping in the battlefields?—that he refuses to go home. David even gets him drunk, but Uriah insists on sleeping outside the palace with the rest of the king's officers.

**LOW POINT:** So David dispatches Uriah back to the frontlines, then orders everyone else to fall back once the fighting gets fierce. It does, they do, and Uriah bites it. Even worse, Bathsheba grieves for, like, two minutes, then hightails it over to the palace, where David's already hired a wedding planner. Long live the king.

> The world's smallest Bible was published in 1895 in Glasgow, Scotland. It contains 520 numbered pages bound by silk thread and is less than a quarter-inch thick. In fact, it could fit in a common tablespoon. If you had the world's tiniest Bible with you while you were eating soup at a restaurant, you could pull the old "Hey, there's a Bible in my soup!" trick and totally freak out the waiter.

## UZZAH

One of Abinadab's sons, which doesn't mean much unless you know that for twenty years, the Ark of the Covenant gets stored in

Abinadab's house in Kiriath Jearim. Then David decides to move it to Jerusalem, which proves unfortunate for Uzzah.

**KEY PASSAGE:** 2 Samuel 6:1–8

**HIGH POINT:** Lives under the same roof as the Ark of the Covenant—the portable chest that represents no less than the presence of God.

**LOW POINT:** Along with his brother, Ahio, Uzzah builds a nice new cart to carry the Ark. They hitch it up to some oxen and start to transport it. Then one of the oxen stumbles, the Ark shifts, and Uzzah—presumably reacting on protective instinct as opposed to malicious intent—reaches out to steady the holy relic of relics, and … dies instantly. Poof.

## WISE MEN, THE

Mysterious kings, astrologers, magi, or noblemen of some sort— honestly, we're not exactly sure *who* these guys are—who wander their way into Matthew's version of the Christmas story. Having followed an eastern star, they show up in Judea in search of the Christ child. After meeting secretly with Herod, they get directions to Bethlehem and eventually arrive to present Jesus with expensive gifts of gold, frankincense, and myrrh. Which, to be honest, are *so* not the most appropriate gifts for a baby.

**KEY PASSAGE:** Matthew 2:1–12

**HIGH POINT:** They become glittery fixtures in future retellings of the Christmas story and nativity displays, even though they don't make an appearance at the manger. No, really, they don't. Matthew 2:11 says they go to the *house* where Jesus lives. These guys may have shown up as late as a year or two after the birth. So your cute little nativity scene that shows the bearded, crowned Wise Men mingling with a bunch of shepherds? A total crock.[11]

---

11. Another crock? The idea that there were only three of them. Matthew doesn't give us a specific number. We assume there were three because they brought three gifts, but you know what they say about assuming.

**LOW POINT:** By informing Herod of the birth of the potential Messiah—and then failing to return to him with a report of the child's whereabouts—the Wise Men inadvertently trigger Herod's slaughter of all boys under two years old in and around Bethlehem (Matt. 2:16). Do us all a favor and try not to bring up this part of the story next Christmas.

## YAHWEH

The creator of the universe, redeemer of mankind, and the Story behind the stories in the Bible. Yahweh is the name by which God identifies himself to Moses via the burning bush. Because it is the sanctified name of the God of Israel, pious Jews from the Babylonian exile onward usually decline from saying it in public reading and will only write its abbreviated version: YHWH. Around the sixteenth century, this develops into the name "Jehovah."

**KEY PASSAGE:** It's pretty much all key.

**HIGH POINT:** Finishes up the whole creation thing on Day Six by fashioning humans in his image, then giving them dominion over plants and animals and birds of the air and fish of the sea and so forth. Then steps back, takes a look at everything, and pronounces it "good." *Very* good. And on Day Seven, Yahweh takes a holiday (Gen. 1:26–2:3).

**LOW POINT:** It's not four chapters later that Adam and Eve are enlisting diet tips from a snake, the Garden's gone to pot, Cain's whacking his brother Abel out in a field, their descendents are turning wickeder and wickeder, and God comes to the conclusion that it would be better to just hose the place down and start over. So He does. Cue the flood. And seven chapters into the Bible, Yahweh takes a mulligan (Gen. 6–9).

## ZACCHAEUS

Zacchaeus was a wee little man, a wee little man was he. / He climbed up in the sycamore tree the Savior for to see. / And as the Savior passed his way, he looked up in the tree. / And said, "Zacchaeus, you come down! For I'm going to your house today. For I'm going to your house today."[12]

**KEY PASSAGE:** Luke 19:1–10

**HIGH POINT:** Inspired by Jesus' willingness to dine with him—a wealthy, despised tax collector and sinner extraordinaire—Zacchaeus promises to give half his stuff to the poor and repay anyone he's cheated four times over.

**LOW POINT:** Thanks to that goofy children's song, known primarily for being a tree-climbing shorty, as opposed to a *generous* tree-climbing shorty. Would it have killed the songwriter to add a second verse about quadruple tax refunds or something?

---

12. In case you're wondering, these are the lyrics to a popular children's song about Zacchaeus. There are hand motions that accompany them, but they're difficult to convey in print.

# WHAT HAPPENS, PART I
## (THE OLD TESTAMENT AT BREAKNECK SPEED)

You know the key terms; you know the key players. So now's a good time to learn what happens when the aforementioned terms and players hook up, starting with the Old Testament. This is where it all begins—literally— and where you'll read a skull-smacking mix of beloved Vacation Bible School-friendly stories (Noah! Jonah! David and Goliath!) and moments of violence and treachery that'll leave you feeling worse than a fat king with a knife in the gut (see **Judges**, below).

So, here's a jittery fast-forward through thousands of years and thousands of pages. If you don't want to know what happens in the Bible, by all means, put this book down and walk away. Because: **SPOILER ALERT.**

## GENESIS

The Old Testament kicks off with a bang. A big one. Because out of a formless void, God creates the heavens and the earth, light and dark, dry land and water, plants and animals, and, eventually, people. In just a few days. He pronounces it "good." Then a serpent shows up in the Garden of Eden and convinces Adam and Eve—the aforementioned people—to disobey God and eat of the tree of the knowledge of good and evil. They do. God pronounces this "bad,"

> **Apples are mentioned in Joel (1:12), Song of Solomon (2:3, 7:8, 8:5), and Proverbs (25:11). But not in the Garden of Eden passages in Genesis.**

and things go downhill from there. Cain kills Abel. Other generations follow, and since these generations aren't any better than Cain's, God decides to start over. He floods the place, destroying everyone but Noah, his family, and a menagerie of doublemint animal pairs. They repopulate the earth once it dries out.

A few of Noah's descendants try to build a tower to heaven, but God's not a fan of the architecture. He confounds the people's languages and spreads everyone out across the earth. Including Abraham, whom God promises to make the father of many nations. Abraham says hello to his son, Isaac. God says goodbye to the wicked cities of Sodom and Gomorrah—and no, not the awesome kind of wicked. This is the traditional wicked, emphasis on the *ick*. Isaac gets rich, finds a wife, and has twins: Jacob and Esau. Esau's not quite the go-getter Jacob becomes, so we don't hear much from him. Jacob, however, wrestles with God, literally, and wins a new name: Israel. He has a bunch of children, the most famous of whom is Joseph. Joseph has a flashy coat. His eleven brothers think he's a prissy little git, so they sell him into slavery. God has other plans, though, and Joseph ends up at the top of Egypt's food chain during a serious famine. Which works out well for his no-account brothers once they come begging for Egyptian table scraps. It's a sweet family reunion, complete with the usual sorry-we-sold-you-into-slavery awkwardness. Jacob eventually dies, and the band of brothers returns to Egypt with Joseph. Then Joseph dies, and Genesis ends.

## EXODUS

The Egyptians eventually forget that Joseph once big-timed it along the Nile, so they turn the growing clan of Israelites into slaves, forcing them to build pyramids and sphinxes and sarcophagi and whatnot. Pharaoh puts an official whack on all the baby Israelite boys, so when Moses is born, his family decides to hide him by shipping him down the Nile in a floating basket. Pharaoh's daughter finds him, adopts him, and Moses comes of age in the royal palace. As an adult, Moses kills a guy he sees knocking around a fellow Israelite. So he goes on the lam. And herds some lambs. One day, all alone out in the desert, he runs into a talking burning bush. The bush tells Moses to meet up with his brother, Aaron—who enters the narrative out of nowhere—and head back to Egypt. Moses agrees to it, but not before asking (and getting answers to) a few questions, as anyone would in a discussion with a fiery plant.

Moses scoots back to Egypt.

> **Moses to Pharaoh:** "Let my people go."
> **Pharaoh to Moses:** "Not by the ritual false beard hanging off my chinny-chin-chin."

Therefore, plagues: blood, frogs, gnats, flies, diseased animals, boils, hail, locusts, darkness, and the particularly nasty death of the firstborn. The first Passover, too.

**Pharaoh to Moses:** "Yeah, okay. Now you can go."

So the Israelites pack up and leave, tracking a big godly cloud during the day and a pillar of fire during the night. Pharaoh instantly regrets his emancipation proclamation and sends a bunch of chariots in pursuit of Israel. They make it to the temporarily parted Red Sea, at which point Pharaoh's army realizes "Swim Like an Egyptian" will never be the title of a hit Bangles song. Unless it's a song about death.

The people get hungry. God feeds them manna, which conveniently plummets from heaven every day. They get into the first of many skirmishes with the Amalekites. During a pit stop at Sinai, God dictates to Moses the Ten Commandments and a bunch of other laws. (Seriously: there's another dozen chapters' worth of Old Testament policy in addition to the Top Ten.) Israel promises to play by the rules. God, in turn, promises to bless them. Moses heads up the mountain to pick up the official signed documents of the Covenant—a couple of stone tablets—but on the way back down he must have taken a wrong turn. Because he ends up at Mardi Gras on the Sinai, where his impatient charges have somehow convinced Aaron to melt down their bling and fashion it into a golden calf, which they're caught worshiping. Dang. Angry and hurt, Moses spikes the tablets. Not known for their bounciness, the tablets crack. God is *not* gonna be happy about that.

Later, Moses gets a peek at God's glory, which makes him glow. God chisels new tablets, then spells out even more rules about the Sabbath and the Ark of the Covenant and the Holy Tent and other important religious paraphernalia. God points them toward Canaan, the land he long ago promised to their forefather Abraham.

## LEVITICUS

After several chapters of rules about various types of offerings, God appoints Aaron and his sons to be priests. They get special uniforms and are put in charge of offering the sacrifices on behalf of the people. And they have to do it the right way, or else they'll die. Exhibit A: Aaron's sons Nadab and Abihu, who forget an important sacrificial step and get fireballed by God. Priesthood is one of those high-pressure, high-reward kinds of positions.

Then the Lord informs Moses and Aaron of more rules. These commands are more pedestrian than the earlier "thou shalt nots." For instance, the Israelites learn what they aren't allowed to eat (eagle, vulture, and stork sandwiches will not be tolerated)[1]; what to do if one's clothing gets all mildewy (a priest has to isolate it, monitor its moldy growth, and, in really bad cases, burn it)[2]; and how to purify yourself if you mistakenly touch something a menstruating woman has sat on (wash your clothes, take a bath, and stay away from everyone else because you're unclean until nightfall).[3] This is fascinating for a few verses, but the tediosity scale tips after about ten chapters. Except for chapter 20, which features a lurid list of sexual no-noes. Leviticus winds down with more rules about appropriate priestly behavior, followed by reminders about promise-keeping and property values. The whole exodus narrative starts to lose a little momentum. Let's move on.

## NUMBERS

All the families and tribes and divisions and camps get counted, hence this book's no-nonsense name. Then God spells out even

1. Leviticus 11:13–19
2. Leviticus 13:47–59
3. Leviticus 15:19–33

more rules. The people get grumbly again because this manna stuff is getting booooring. They've got a hankering for protein. So God provides, chasing an obscene amount of quail into camp. The Israelites fire up the grill, but everyone who takes the first meaty bite gets some sort of horrible mouth disease. The whiniest of the whiners die. Manna, anyone?

Moses sends spies into Canaan to scout the inhabitants of the Promised Land. Moses wants to know: *These Canaanites ... can we take 'em?* The spooks come in from the cold and answer with a big fat "no." Not unless Moses gets his jollies by reaching up and slugging giants in the knee. Or lobbing sand grenades at walled fortresses.

There are two dissenters, Spy Caleb and Spy Joshua, who are blessed with more courage and faith than the others. "Sure, they're big and bad," they announce, "but we've got God on our side."

No one hears this sensible pronouncement, due to a new round of complaining. A few of the Israelites even start getting all nostalgic about Egypt, home of the sparkling Nile, balmy weather, hot meals, and those postcard-worthy pyramids.[4]

God's had enough. He proclaims that none of the complainers will get to cross the threshold into the Promised Land. None. End of discussion. Every last one of them will die in the desert. Annoyed, a guy named Korah leads his family and friends in an uprising against Moses. God responds with an uprising of his own, and Korah gets swallowed up by, well, a big hole in the ground. God's serious about this dying-in-the-desert thing. Not long after, Moses loses his cool, too, mishandling his God-power by smacking a rock in frustration with his walking stick. Water gushes out miraculously, but God punishes Moses for his arrogance. No Promised Land for you, either, Gramps. To top it off, Aaron dies.

4. Which, of course, they helped *build*. As slaves. Good thinkin', Israel.

A bit of warfare commences. Balaam enters the picture for a few chapters and has a brief but entertaining conversation with his donkey.[5] Israelite men get busy with local Moabite women and end up worshiping Baal. God is not amused and afflicts them with a nasty strain of the God flu. Thousands die. Eventually, so does Moses. But not before God puts Moses' first lieutenant, Joshua the Optimistic Spy, in charge. And not before God instructs Israel to cross the Jordan, stomp right into Canaan, and claim the territory for themselves. Giants and walled cities be damned. Literally. Because ... God.

## DEUTERONOMY

Right there in the blowing sands of the desert, east of the Jordan River, Moses addresses the people one last time prior to entering Canaan. (Also one last time prior to dying, though in this book we don't officially know that yet.) And the first thirty chapters are the entire text

> In ancient Israel, a man could divorce his wife for the crime of becoming "displeasing" to him on account of him discovering "something undecent about her" (Deut. 24:1). A wife couldn't divorce her husband for any reason.

of this speech. Lots of: *remember when we did this?* And plenty of: *listen to the commands of the Lord.* One of the high points comes in chapter 6, a passage known as the *Shema Yisrael*, which begins with this well-known commandment: "Hear, O Israel: The Lord our God, the Lord is one. Love the Lord your God with all your heart and with all your soul and with all your strength."[6]

After the speech ends, Moses introduces Joshua as the new leader. He encourages Joshua to be strong and courageous, and then breaks into song. No lie. It's called the "Song of Moses," and don't let

---

5. Read it for yourself in Numbers 22.
6. Deuteronomy 6:4–5. The *Shema* is considered the most important prayer in Judaism and still plays a central role in almost all Jewish prayer services. Jesus quotes it in Mark 12:29–30 when asked what is the most important commandment.

anyone tell you it's not a little catchy.[7] Then he hikes up Mount Nebo, blesses the people of Israel, and dies within sight of the Promised Land.

> In the King James, this verse from Joshua 7:24—"And Joshua, and all Israel with him, took Achan the son of Zerah, and the silver, and the garment, and the wedge of gold, and his sons, and his daughters, and his oxen, and his asses, and his sheep, and his tent, and all that he had: and they brought them unto the valley of Achor"— contains every letter of the alphabet except for Q. If only Achan had quail instead of asses ...

## JOSHUA

God hands over the wheel of the exodus bus into Joshua's capable hands. First stop? The big, scary walled city of Jericho. But don't worry, because God promises to personally force out the current inhabitants. Which sucks for them, but makes things considerably easier for Israel. Joshua sends spies into Jericho. They hide in the home of the prostitute Rahab. (Yes, holing up under a prostitute's bed sounds pretty convenient, but let's give these devout Jewish boys the benefit of the doubt.)

All of Israel crosses the Jordan River with a little Red Sea–style panache, thanks to a miraculous stopping of the current. Then God unveils for Joshua his secret weapon for toppling the impenetrable stronghold of Jericho.

It's ... marching.

Parade the Ark of the Covenant around the city for a whole week, God tells them, with extra marching and yelling and horn-blowing on Day Seven. Israel obeys, and it works. The walls crumble. Israel wins in a rout. Later, in a more conventional non-

---

7. Sample lyric: "I will send wasting famine against them, / consuming pestilence and deadly plague; / I will send against them the fangs of wild beasts, / the venom of vipers that glide in the dust" (Deut. 32:24).

marching/yelling/blowing conquest, Israel takes on the king of Ai and wins. Soon after, a gang of wily Gibeonites shows up all rag-tag and whimpery and tricks Joshua into making a peace agreement with them. Then Israel attacks the Amorites. At some point during the battle, Joshua uses the power of God to unleash a killer wartime strategy—seriously, why has no one else ever thought of this?—and prayerfully commands the sun to stand still for twenty-four hours, thus prolonging daylight, which is more conducive to brutal bloodletting than nighttime. And Joshua's bending of the time-space continuum? Pretty effective. Anyway, more defeating of kings and native peoples follows. Conquered land gets distributed among the Israelites. Joshua dies, but not before reminding them again of the Law and the importance of not worshiping false gods.

## JUDGES

Having conquered most of the Canaanites, Israel backs up the trucks and starts unpacking in the long-awaited Promised Land. They organize themselves as a loose confederation of tribes. And though they've officially staked their claim on God's property, they don't just up and force everyone to leave. Because that would be mean. Instead, Israel forces all of the native stragglers into a quaint institution called slavery. And, yes, there are some ironies in that fire.

The next generation of Israelites gets so loaded on the free-flowing milk and honey that they forget about God. Which ain't too hard when you're plastering your tent walls with posters of third-string Canaanite deities like Baal and Ashtoreth. Like a jilted lover, God removes his blessing, and the leftover Canaanite squatters rise up and wreak havoc on Israel. So God recruits a judge—more John Wayne than Judge Judy—to save them from their enemies. It becomes a pattern. Idolatry ... trouble ... judgment ... repentance ... idolatry. Over and over again for the next four centuries.

A few judges get more biblical props than others. There's Ehud, who knifes the fat king of Moab in an obesely yucky story.[8] And Deborah, the only female judge, whose nemesis gets nailed to the ground with a tent stake through the head.[9] Gideon gets a visit from the angel of the Lord, tears down idols, tests God with sheepskin, and defeats hundreds of thousands of his enemies with a slapdash gang of three hundred trumpet-blowing, jar-smashing soldiers. Tola, son of Dodo, does nothing worth mentioning but has an awesome name.[10] Jephthah defeats the Ammonites and makes a horrible promise to God that requires him to sacrifice his one and only daughter.[11] And, finally, Samson earns a name for himself with a killer combination of long hair, super-strength, wicked battle skills, and Delilah lust.

Other judges—including Jair of Gilead, Ibzan of Bethlehem, Elon of Zebulun, and Abdon of Ephraim—get listed but aren't noteworthy. The book closes with a delightful story about a Levite whose servant girl gets gang-raped and killed by the Benjamites of Gilead. So the Levite chops her up limb by limb and FedExes the twelve individual pieces across the land. It's a violent, disturbing end to a violent, disturbing book. Slap an "adults only" label on this one.

# RUTH

A nice, short, lovey-dovey, carnage-free book, which is a definite relief at this point in the narrative. Set during the period of the judges, it tells how a childless Moabite widow named Ruth travels to Judah with her mother-in-law, Naomi.[12] There, they meet

8. Judges 3:12–30
9. Judges 4:17–22
10. Judges 10:1–2
11. Judges 11:29–40
12. This is a crazy thing to do, as Ruth owes her (former) mother-in-law nothing after Ruth's husband dies. In fact, Naomi tells her to return to her original home, but Ruth is really nice and decides to stay.

Boaz, a nice, regular guy who takes Ruth as his wife. Together they have a son. Everyone's happy, including the formerly grandchildless Naomi. Oh, and their son? He's named Obed. Father of Jesse. Grandfather of David. From whose lineage comes Jesus Christ.

# 1 & 2 SAMUEL

In a nutshell, Israel gets a powerful judge/prophet (Samuel), a mediocre king (Saul), and finally, a good king (David). Here's how it goes down. God calls Samuel as a child, and he grows up to lead Israel. Then Israel—seeing how all its enemies have kings—decides it needs a certified crown-wearer of its own.

> **People:** (chanting) "We want a king! A ring-a-ding-ding!"
> **Samuel:** "God? These folks want a king, apparently, and they're rhyming about it. Your thoughts?"
> **God:** "You're about to meet up with a guy looking for donkeys. He's tall. Sign him up."

And so Samuel meets Saul, who stands a head taller than anyone else in Israel. And, yes, he's out looking for his father's donkeys, for whatever reason. So Samuel appoints Saul as king, then casually bows out of the public eye. Saul gets an immediate injection of the Spirit of God and does some cool things, like winning important battles and exhibiting superior decision making under pressure. Then he falls off the obedience wagon. God rejects Saul as king, and the Lord's Spirit departs from him.

A shepherd boy moves into the neighborhood. David kills Goliath the Philistine with a well-placed rock. Saul gets nervous.

David marries Saul's daughter, and as a wedding gift for the father of the bride, David brings Saul the foreskins of two hundred conquered Philistines. Not that Saul is overly impressed, because soon after unwrapping the thoughtful gift, he tries to pin David and his pretty-boy harp to the wall with a spear. Welcome to the family. David flees. Saul pursues with murderous rage. One night, David gets a once-in-Methusaleh's-lifetime chance to kill Saul but refuses to lay so much as a big toe on "the Lord's anointed."[13] Saul's less worried about executing anyone's anointed, because after being gravely wounded in a subsequent battle, he takes his own life by falling on his sword.[14]

David becomes king over the southern tribes of Judah, while Saul's son Ish-Bosheth takes charge of the rest of Israel. There's a long war between the supporters of Saul's family and those of David. Finally Saul Jr. dies and David gains control over all of Israel. He wins lots of wars. He brings the Ark back to Jerusalem.[15] He pulls a peeping Dave on Bathsheba, has his royal way with her, gets her husband capped, then starts addressing wedding invitations. Eventually, these two have a son named Solomon. More warfare and conquering. David clashes with another son named Absalom, who rebels and tries to usurp the throne, but this works itself out when Absalom dies at the hand of David's commander-in-chief, Joab, in one of history's most amusing death scenes. Long hair and an oak tree are involved.[16] Later, the Lord smites Israel with disease, and to stop this, David buys a threshing floor and builds an altar to the Lord there. God answers his prayers, and we move on to ...

13. 1 Samuel 26:9
14. 1 Samuel 31:4
15. A brief history of the Ark's time away from Israel: The Philistines take possession of it after defeating Israel at Ebenezer (1 Sam. 4:1–11). But it mystically topples their deity statues and inflicts the people with nasty boils and rashes, so they slap a return label on the mercy seat and ship it back. After stopovers in the homes of Abinadab and Obed-Edom, David parades it back to Jerusalem.
16. Absalom's death is one of the more creative ones in the Bible, and that's saying a lot. Read about it in 2 Samuel 18:9–33.

# 1 & 2 KINGS

David dies, and Solomon gets fitted for the throne. And no sooner does he jam his can into the royal seat than God grants Solomon a heap o' wisdom. Why? Primarily because Solomon has the good sense to ask for it. He builds a temple so Israel can worship God all proper and everything, and we get meticulous details about its construction. It takes seven years for Solomon's crew to complete it; much of their time is apparently spent carving pomegranates into the woodwork.[17] Finally the Ark is delivered to the Temple, and sacrifices resume there. Much rejoicing.

Solomon also erects a mongo palace for himself, and this structure takes thirteen years to finish. One would think a truly wise individual might rethink the decision to put twice as much effort into *his* home than God's home, but no one seems too bothered by this.

> Of all the woven containers mentioned in the Bible, baskets were perhaps the most versatile for carrying people. A medium-sized basket transported baby Moses down the Nile (Exod. 2:3). A large, person-sized basket helped Saul escape from Damascus (Acts 9:25). And seventy small baskets were just the right size for the decapitated heads of the seventy sons of Ahab (2 Kings 10:7).

Meanwhile, Solomon ain't just doing construction; he's also planning weddings. A lot. He ties the knot with some seven hundred wives—in addition to three hundred concubines—and not all of them are from Israel. The result is that Solomon gets a sizeable at-home injection of pagan religion. God's not so down with this, as might be expected, so he stirs up Solomon's enemies. But

God can't bring himself to completely lay waste to Israel, because David was such a great king, so he keeps his promises. Solomon's kingdom stays intact. Until he dies.

At which point the kingdom splits apart faster than a hot celebrity couple with a cutesy nickname. Solomon's son Rehoboam succeeds him, but pretty much only the people of Judah—the southern part of the nation—like him. The northerners? Not so much. The rest of Israel decides to elect their own king, a guy named Jeroboam. (And yes, the names are similar, and it gets very confusing. Deal with it.) So one big monarchy morphs into two smallish, weak, divided kingdoms. A bunch of sorry kings succeed Jeroboam, and God has to send his prophet, Elijah, to straighten them out. Elijah's got sweet prophecy game and is generally a gnat in the ear of evil kings like Ahab. And when Elijah dies, his assistant Elisha is right there to pick up the slack.

Not that it helps. After a whole succession of sorry leadership, Israel gets attacked by Assyria and deported to parts unknown. Assyrian carpetbaggers lay claim to Samaria and—just like that—the Northern Kingdom's gone. Meanwhile, Judah has its own difficulties with an equally bad streak of kings, until Hezekiah takes the throne. He successfully resists the still-marauding Assyrians. Then we get more kings and more disobedience until Nebuchadnezzar, king of Babylon, knocks on Judah's door. He's selling an industrial dose of Persian beatdown. The Babylonian army surrounds Jerusalem, busts through the walls, lays waste to the Temple, and carts the Jewish inhabitants eastward as captives. Welcome, children of Israel, to the Babylonian exile.

# I & 2 CHRONICLES

*Déjà vu*. The first book starts off with a flourish worthy of

Numbers, listing out a whole mess of names: a genealogy from Adam to David, a catalog of kings and Temple musicians, and a register of returned exiles and their families. Nine chapters' worth. Then we get a quick recap of the death of Saul and some highlights of David's reign as king, along with more names: priests, gatekeepers, tribal leaders, and directors of various divisions of David's kingdom.[18]

Guess what's next? Yep, a recap of Solomon's administration. Then the whole Jeroboam/Rehoboam divided kingdom brainteaser sets in, followed by several chapters devoted to the military exploits and misdeeds of the rest of the kings of Judah (2 Chron. 11–36). In the closing chapter, Nebuchadnezzar arrives. Jerusalem falls. Seventy years of exile, captivity, and slavery in Babylon commence. But wait! Two verses from the end of 2 Chronicles, we finally get a new scoop. Cyrus takes over as king of Persia. He sends out a memo to the whole kingdom. Its message? People of Israel … you're free to go.

## EZRA

Details emerge on King Cyrus' emancipation declaration. He frees up a caravan-load of Jerusalem's plunder, so the captives end up trucking back their own cattle and silver and dishes and stuff. They resettle in their hometowns and get to work rebuilding the altar and the Temple. But next door, trouble's brewing. The hated Samaritans (who snatched up all the open real estate after Assyria pillaged the Northern Kingdom) aren't exactly throwing a "welcome home" party for their new neighbors. Once Cyrus dies and Artaxerxes takes his place, the Samaritans post a letter to Persia tattling on the Jerusalem goings-on. Comedy ensues.

---

18. The list of directors is a fascinating one, because only here do we find out that Jehdeiah, from Meronoth, is in charge of the king's donkeys (1 Chron. 27:30).

**Samaritans:** *Dearest and most handsome King Artaxerxes: All these people showed up in Jerusalem, and now they're rebuilding the Temple and the city walls and, dear oh dear, they'll probably incorporate and stop paying taxes. We thought you should know. You're awesome.*

**Artaxerxes:** *Thanks for the letter. My files indicate that Jerusalem is a royal pain. Plus, their tax money keeps all these hanging gardens afloat. Tell them to stop.*

Construction stops. Artaxerxes dies. Darius becomes king of Persia. Construction starts up again. The nosy neighbors send another letter.

**Samaritans:** *King Darius! They're doing it again! We tried to stop them from rebuilding the Temple, but they keep saying Cyrus gave them permission. You'd better check your archives and prove them wrong. Also, you rock.*

**Darius:** *Now listen up, you whiny snotlickers. I did check the records, and Cyrus did order them to rebuild the Temple. And the whole thing's on my credit card! So lay off. Bother them any more, and I'll have the authorities pull a wooden beam from the walls of your house and impale you with it.[19] LOL!*

The Temple gets completed. The returned captives celebrate Passover. The rest of the book is about Ezra, a priest/scribe who shows up to scold the Jewish men for not marrying Jewish women. It's less interesting than the letter writing.

# NEHEMIAH

Additional details about the rebuilding of Jerusalem's walls.

19. This is an actual threat, from Ezra 6:11.

Nehemiah gets permission from Artaxerxes to return to Jerusalem as governor. The deteriorated walls distress him, so he takes charge of the renovation. Despite the occasional plot against his work crew from attack-minded Samaritan neighbors, construction finishes around chapter 6. Ezra puts in an appearance and reads the Law to everyone, and this is followed by a day of penance and prayer. Good call, Ezra. The prayer holiday is followed, at least in the book of Nehemiah, by a smattering of lists, the dedication of the wall, administrative particulars, and the same intrigue about mixed marriages.

## ESTHER

A tense little Babylonian captivity story. King Xerxes gets rid of his wife, Queen Vashti, because she refuses to participate in a check-out-my-smokin'-wife show for visiting VIPs. So Xerxes puts on a beauty pageant to locate the next missus.

> The eunuch Shaashgaz is mentioned one time in the book of Esther. God is mentioned zero times in the book of Esther.

A secretly Jewish girl named Esther—who's been raised by her cousin, Mordecai—wins the contest. She and Mordecai foil a plot against the king (which is good). One of the king's employees, a scab named Haman, gets promoted to chief officer (which is bad). Haman gets all uppity about his new title and commands Mordecai to bow to him. Mordecai, a faithful Jew, will have none of that. So Haman, in a fit of rage, tricks Xerxes into signing a decree to kill all Jewish people. Uh-oh. Then Haman erects a gallows to give Mordecai his due, just because the dude gives him the furies.

But wait! King Xerxes wants to honor Mordecai for saving

his life by foiling the aforementioned sinister plot, so he tells Officer Haman to organize a parade for his arch-nemesis. Burn. Then Esther tells the king about her Jewishness and Haman's dirty decree-scheming, and Xerxes orders Haman hanged on the very gallows he assembled for Mordecai. Double burn! To commemorate the deliverance, the Jews celebrate the inaugural feast of Purim.[20]

# JOB

Job is wealthy, happy, and faithful to God. This results in a cosmic exchange of smack between God and Satan, and God's all, "Check out my faithful servant, Job." To which Satan replies, "So? Job's only faithful because you're blessing him. Let me curse him instead, and he'll spit in your face."

And, weirdly, God agrees to the contest. He hands his pious servant over to the devil, who's allowed to do anything short of killing him. So Satan kills other stuff. Job's thousands of cattle, sheep, camels, and donkeys fall over dead. His servants die. A tornado tears through a house, and all of Job's sons and daughters die, too. And to make things worse, Satan smites Job with a painful skin disease. Job sits down amid the ruins of his nicely manicured life and scratches his boils with a pottery shard. Mrs. Job advises him to curse God and die. Job refuses.

His friends Eliphaz, Bildad, and Zophar pop in and start forcing Job to listen to a bunch of speeches with a singular theme: sucks about all the trauma, Job, but it's pretty much your own fault. Job protests his innocence and challenges God to explain why all this bad stuff is happening to a him. Another friend, Elihu, adds a couple more speeches at the end in defense of God. And then God himself takes the stage, speaking out of a whirlwind. He

20. Named after the lots (Hebrew: *Pûr*) Haman cast to determine the day and month of the planned genocide (Esther 3:7).

belittles Job's buddies, vindicates Job for his innocence, and ends up restoring everything Job lost, and then some. Presumably, Satan learns a very valuable lesson.

## PSALMS

A collection of 150 prayers, poems, and songs of faith—many of which are written by David—much beloved by Bible readers because they express the whole enchilada of human experience. There are joyful psalms about how wonderful God is, despairing psalms about God's apparent abandonment of the psalmist, and violent psalms about God breaking the teeth of the wicked.[21] A little something for everybody.

This is the kind of poetry even non-English majors can get into, because who doesn't take comfort in, for example, Psalm 23 ("Even though I walk through the valley of the shadow of death, I will fear no evil, for you are with me") or Psalm 30 ("His anger lasts only a moment, but his favor lasts a lifetime")?[22]

Far and away one of the best parts of the Bible. But not much in terms of storyline.

## PROVERBS

An assorted collection of clever sayings and acrostic poems about all kinds of everyday stuff, mostly attributed to the super wise Solomon. Example: "He who winks with his eye is plotting perversity; he who purses his lips is bent on evil."[23]

Steer clear, then, of kissy-faced winkers.

## ECCLESIASTES

An advice manual, traditionally attributed to Solomon, which reflects on the meaning of life, the limitations of human existence,

21. Psalm 3:7
22. Psalm 23:4, Psalm 30:5
23. Proverbs 16:30

and the mystery of God's ways. Its main theme—that the fleeting nature of mankind's existence makes life meaningless, even senseless—gives the book a real up-with-people sort of vibe.

## SONG OF SOLOMON

You have to wonder how this book made the canon, because it's not much more than an explicit dose of ancient erotic poetry. Lots of theologians have tried to approach it allegorically—yo, all that breast-fondling stuff is apparently about God's love for his bride, the Church!—but that gets a little awkward. In a cosmological sense.

So we're left with what amounts to the Hebrew *Kama Sutra*, starring Solomon and his nubile lover. For kicks, here's a lyrical sample, spoken by the female: "Let my lover come into his garden / and taste its choice fruits."[24] Uh ... her "garden"? Not really a garden.

*Bomp-chicka-bow-wow.*

## ISAIAH

Still no real narrative to follow. Isaiah is a compilation of prophetic speeches from the book's namesake to the people of Jerusalem and Judah, pre-exile. It kicks off with a big-time slam as Isaiah compares Judah to Sodom and warns of the coming judgment against God's people (chapters 2–12). Then comes a whole slate of judgment due foreign peoples like the Babylonians and Assyrians (chapters 13–23). And another smidge of judgment against, well, everyone else (chapters 24–27). Possibly fatigued from all the doomsaying, the author takes a break in chapters 36–39 to

> You probably think there is no mention of cucumbers in the Bible, but you're wrong, thanks to Isaiah 1:8.

recap the Hezekiah story from 2 Kings 18–20. The rest of the book focuses on the Babylon situation, promising Israel's deliverance from its captives and anticipating eventual restoration.[25] The Persian king Cyrus gets special attention as one of God's chosen instruments, as does someone referred to as the "suffering servant," mentioned in chapters 42, 49, 50, 52, and 53—which most Christians believe to be a selection of prophecies about the coming Messiah, fulfilled in Jesus Christ. Jews are less enthusiastic about this interpretation. Because of all the Messianic prophecies, however, Isaiah gets quoted extensively in the New Testament.

> The longest name in the Bible is Mahershalalhashbaz. God tells the prophet Isaiah to give his son this name in Isaiah 8:3. It means "quick to the plunder, swift to the spoil." You know it's bad when you can define the name faster than you can pronounce it.

## JEREMIAH

More oracles against Judah and Jerusalem, specifically about the reigns of Josiah, Jehoiakim, and Zedekiah. Here comes the imminent destruction, yada yada yada. This is followed by a whole section of autobiographical stuff about Jeremiah, mainly about how hard it is to be him during the Babylonian siege of Jerusalem—which he predicts. And which gets him charged with treason by Zedekiah and thrown in jail. Once Jerusalem actually falls, Jeremiah gets paroled. Mainly because all the stuff he said would happen ends up happening. Jeremiah jets off for Egypt with a bunch of other Jewish escapees, where he continues to prophesy about

---

25. So, you're wondering, how can this have been written pre-exile, yet still refer to specific events from the Babylonian exile? You're not alone. Many scholars hypothesize either (a) multiple authorship, with at least one guy (Isaiah) covering chapters 1–39 and another writer tacking on the rest at a later date; or (b) heavy editing after Isaiah's first draft. Others hypothesize (c) God-inspired prophecy.

coming disaster. The book closes with a selection of better-watch-out messages to foreign nations and a final narrative of the fall of Jerusalem.

## LAMENTATIONS

A sad little five-chapter dirge about the decline of Jerusalem and its destruction by Babylon. Traditionally authored by Jeremiah, an idea we get from 2 Chronicles 35:25, which mentions him writing some "laments." But this is disputed.

## EZEKIEL

One of the Babylonian exiles, Ezekiel starts the ball rolling with a trippy introduction involving winged creatures with human hands and cow hooves and some sort of fiery composition. Each monster has four faces—a human face, a lion face, an ox face, and an eagle face. They're accompanied by some flashy spinning wheels. Wheels with eyes. Upon seeing this stuff, surrounded by flashes of lightning and a rainbow-colored glow coming from a human-shaped Something sitting on a throne, Ezekiel hears a voice and receives a scroll. He's told to eat the scroll, then vomit up its contents to the people of Israel. No, really. The rest of the book consists of these regurgitations—oracles against Jerusalem and its neighbors, hope for future restoration, and even plans for a reconstructed Temple—punctuated by several more visions, ecstatic trances, and even wacked-out performance art.[26]

> Random biblical phrase out of context: "You will keep your turbans on your heads and your sandals on your feet" (Ezek. 24:23).

---

26. Among other vivid illustrations, Ezekiel brick-maps the fall of Jerusalem (4:1–3), lies on his side for a couple of years (4:4–17), shaves his head and beard (5:1–17), and tunnels through the walls of his house (12:1–16). For various symbolic reasons.

## DANIEL

Hey! A story! Among the young, handsome, well-educated Israelite men dispatched to Babylon by King Nebuchadnezzar are guys named Daniel, Shadrach, Meshach, and Abednego. They stick to a healthy Jewish diet (despite their lavish surroundings) and end up particularly wise. So the king makes them special officers of the court. Then Nebuchadnezzar has a crazy dream. Daniel interprets it, earning himself a lofty position over all the wise men of Babylon. Eventually, the king gets a little too fond of himself and erects a huge, probably-overcompensating-for-something, gold statue for everyone to worship. The devout Shadrach, Meshach, and Abednego refuse to break the first two of the Ten Commandments and, as a result, get tossed into a blazing furnace. The furnace is so hot that the tossers get toasted. But the three nice young men don't even singe their eyebrows. And Nebuchadnezzar catches sight of a fourth guy not getting burned along with them. And this one? He's sorta shiny. Impressive.

The king has another dream, and Daniel interprets: God thinks Nebuchadnezzar has become too powerful and needs to be cranked down a notch. As usual, Daniel rocks the explanation, and the dream comes true when the king suddenly goes apeshiznit and carves out a seven-year *My Side of the Mountain*[27] existence out in the wild, munching grass and growing his hair long. Then he worships God and becomes king again.

Time passes. Much later, Nebuchadnezzar's descendant, King Belshazzar, is partying with his royal guests and wives when a disembodied hand pops out of the ether and starts scribbling on the wall.[28] Belshazzar turns to Daniel for an explanation. Daniel

27. The classic children's book by Jean Craighead George, in which little Sam Gribley runs away from home to live on his own in the Catskill Mountains, where he makes friends with a falcon and a weasel. It's awesome.
28. The hand writes this cryptic message: "*Mene, mene, tekel, parsin.*" According to Daniel, it means Belshazzar's kingdom is about to be handed over to his enemies. But you have to squint to get even that.

interprets the ghost-hand weirdness, gets another promotion, and Belshazzar dies that very night. Darius becomes king and puts Daniel in charge of even more stuff, which makes Daniel's colleagues all jealous. So they draft a bogus law about not praying to any god or human other than the king. Daniel, still a good Jew, disobeys. In public. So Darius reluctantly upholds the law and locks up Daniel in a den of hungry lions. But no worries. God shuts the big cats' big mouths. Daniel survives, Darius responds to the miracle by worshiping God, and everyone's happy.[29]

> "Bible reading is an education in itself."
> —Alfred Lord Tennyson
> (1809–1892)

These much-beloved stories are followed by a bunch of freaky apocalyptic prophecies involving monstrous beasts rising out of the sea, cryptic discussions with the angel Gabriel, and a spate of possible Antichrist imagery that gets End-Times aficionados really hot and bothered.

## HOSEA

God commands the prophet Hosea to hook up with Gomer, a prostitute who's the very definition of unfaithfulness. This is because God wants to use the Hosea-Gomer marriage as a metaphor for his relationship with the spiritually skanky Israel. But Hosea loves his skeeze of a wife anyway, and—good news—so does God.

## JOEL

"Um, Israel?" says the prophet Joel. "The day of the Lord is extremely nigh. So shape up." Also, keep your eyes peeled for a devastating plague of locusts, which may or may not be allegorical,

---

29. Everyone but the men who accused Daniel in the first place. They get tossed into the den too, along with their wives and children. And this time, God declines to break out the cat muzzles.

followed by a war-to-end-all-wars between God and the nations of the world. Which, we're hoping, is all kinds of allegorical.

## AMOS

It's hard to take seriously a sheepherder who ditches his flocks to hitch a ride on the doom-and-gloom train. Even harder when the shepherd's name is Amos, which is *so* not scary. Anyhow, Amos busts out some prophecy during the pre-exile reigns of Judah's King Uzziah and Israel's Jeroboam II. He's mainly peeved about social injustice—the oppression of the poor and a widening economic gap—which he links to Israel's abandonment of God. In other words, judgment's a-coming. Locusts may or may not be involved.

## OBADIAH

The shortest book in the Old Testament. Its one chapter is about—drum roll—the coming judgment of the Lord. But this time it's against Edom. Whew.

## JONAH

God calls Jonah to preach against the evil city of Ninevah. Jonah laces up his jogging shoes and tries to outrun the voice of God. Um, Jonah? No one's that fast. Not even the prostitute Gomer. (*Rimshot!*)

Jonah hops a boat to Tarshish, but God's still tracking him. The Lord stirs up a big storm. Jonah's boat-mates clue in to Jonah as the source of the general wind-and-waviness and heave him into the deep. Luckily, a great fish/whale/allegorical stand-in is there to catch him, and Jonah spends three squishy days in Moby's belly before repenting. Upon hearing the confession, God supplies the fish with a dose of holy castor oil, and Jonah gets vomited back onto dry land. He proceeds to Ninevah, gives the city a good prophetic tongue-lashing, and Ninevah repents. Easy!

You'd think this would make Jonah happy, on account of how he just brought a whole evil city to faith in God. But, no, Jonah mainly gets annoyed. Turns out he's hoping for a display of heavenly wrath. God scolds him for lacking compassion. Then God gives Jonah a nice plant. A worm eats it.[30]

## MICAH

Threats of doom. Promises of salvation. And, at some point in the future, a Messianic king from the lineage of David.[31]

## NAHUM

Jonah hints at it, but here we get a full picture of the wickedness of Ninevah, and it's a virtual Evilpalooza. Whorish, violent, witchcrafty. So Nahum passes along a poetic taunt from God. It describes the Almighty (a) ravaging the city in a Tarantino-esque bloodbath, and (b) exposing Ninevah's hoo-hah in a symbolically naughty peep show. *Oh, no, he did-n't!* Oh, yes, he did. The *Pocket Guide* references Nahum 3:5—"I will lift your skirts over your face. / I will show the nations your nakedness / and the kingdoms your shame." Zing.

## HABAKKUK

Pre-exile, the prophet Habakkuk complains about violence and evil. God answers with a prediction involving Babylonian conquest. Habakkuk tees up the questioning a second time: *Seriously, God? Punish Israel with Babylonians? They're worse than we are!* God answers by drawing up a list of woes directed toward Babylon. *Don't worry, Habakkuk,* says Yahweh. *They'll get their comeuppance, too. Meanwhile,*

30. God digs the metaphor (Jon. 4).
31. Micah 5:2–5

*buck up and be more righteous. It's better for you in the long run.*

Then Habakkuk writes a psalm about God's power.

## ZEPHANIAH

Right before the fall of Jerusalem, during the reign of Josiah, Zephaniah starts singing the familiar song of the minor prophets: coming judgment, glorious future. The tune is catchy enough, but the verses get repetitive.

## HAGGAI

Haggai makes four pronouncements after the Israelites' return from exile in Babylon: (1) Stop messing with your own houses and get to work restoring the Temple. Like, now. (2) No, this Temple probably won't have as many carved pomegranates as the flashy one Solomon built, but quit stressing. We don't have that kind of cash. (3) Pay attention to ritual cleanliness, and God will up the blessing. (4) Zerubbabel's gonna get a promotion, which is of little interest to you Israelites but is a major nod to the Davidic line of leadership. Not to mention a hint at the coming Messianic kingdom.

## ZECHARIAH

One of Haggai's prophetic contemporaries who leans more toward the crazy Ezekiel vein than the prophecies-we-might-actually-understand vein. The following are creatively employed: horses, myrtle trees, horns, measuring sticks, high priests, cameos by both Joshua and Satan (!), a lampstand, a thirty-foot flying scroll, a wicked woman in a basket, four chariots, two shepherds, a stick named "Favor,"[32] and sundry doominess. Discuss amongst yourselves.

---

32. Or "Pleasantness," or "Beauty," depending on your translation (Zech. 11:10).

## MALACHI

The Old Testament caboose chugs into the station. Malachi pronounces oracles on six topics: God's love for his people, disrespectful priests, the trouble caused by mixed marriages, the coming day of judgment, the need for people to repent and start tithing,[33] and the importance of obedience to God. The last verse warns that God will beam Elijah back to town to encourage parents to love their children and children to love their parents. Otherwise, curses aplenty. So get with it, moms, dads, and kids.[34]

> **Random biblical phrase out of context: "Behold, I will corrupt your seed, and spread dung upon your faces" (Mal. 2:3, KJV).**

---

33. The biblical practice of voluntarily returning one-tenth of your income to God by handing it over to the religious leaders.
34. Malachi 4:6

# WHAT HAPPENS, PART 2
## (THE NEW TESTAMENT AT BREAKNECK SPEED)

Most of the violence is over once the Old Testament closes down. The conquering and Temple building and prophetic performance art shut off completely. Instead, we get a generous helping of the life of Christ, a smidge of early Christianity, and some heavy Pauline theology. Not to mention a killer dose of apocalyptic hellfire and freaky metaphor there at the end.

Welcome, ancient travelers, to the New Testament.

## MATTHEW, MARK, LUKE, JOHN

Malachi hits newsstands and then nothing happens, biblically speaking, for about four hundred years. Until a demure, faithful, unmarried Nazarene girl gives birth to Jesus, in the dust and grime of a barn. And without question, this little story becomes the entire focus of the Bible. Sure, Jesus turns out to be the fulfillment of certain prophecies, but he's also the fulfillment of the entire Levitical law itself—the sacrifices, the holiness rules, the commandments. The symbolism of the ark (of Noah) and the Ark (of the Covenant) point to this kid in the manger. Abraham's near-sacrifice of Isaac? Esther's role in saving the Jews? The insane violence of the book of Judges? All are ingredients in this one final, tasty dessert.

After fielding a visit from some Magi and being raised by Mary and her carpenter husband, Joseph, Jesus tiptoes into the limelight. How? By asking his cousin, John, to baptize him in the Jordan River. John obliges, and as Jesus resurfaces, a heavenly public address announcement makes it clear that this guy is special. God then leads Jesus into the wilderness for a forty-day fast, at the end of which Satan shows up and taps out a tempting little song-and-dance number. He offers up power and prestige, but Jesus politely declines. Thus begins his public ministry. Jesus earns a party-person rep at a wedding by turning jugs of water into some downright palatable wine. He picks a bunch of unimpressive nobodies—uneducated fishermen, a zealot or two, a hated tax collector—to be his disciples. Then he gets serious about the preaching, teaching, and healing.

> **The shortest verse in the Bible is John 11:35: "Jesus wept."**

He performs miracles (feeding five thousand men with the contents of a single meal, walking on water, raising his friend Lazarus from the dead).[1] He tells stories (the prodigal son, the good Samaritan, the workers in the vineyard).[2] In the Sermon on the Mount, he teaches a

---

1. The well-known "loaves and fishes" story can be found in all four Gospels. The most detailed account is Mark 6:30–44. Jesus walks on water in Matthew 14:22–33. The resurrection of Lazarus comes from John 11:1–44.

2. The parable of the prodigal son comes from Luke 15:11–32; the good Samaritan, Luke 10:30–37; the workers in the vineyard, Matthew 20:1–16.

revolutionary code of ethics (turn the other cheek, love your enemies, rejoice in your suffering).[3] And he takes potshots at the ruling religious class by healing on the Sabbath, hanging out with drunks and prostitutes, and presuming to speak for God himself. In three years of ministry, Jesus packs it in.

He's a spear in the side of the establishment, though, and before long, the high priests are enlisting a member of his crew—Judas, the group's treasurer and unofficial malcontent—to plot against him. Eventually, Jesus and his followers share a Last Supper together. (Though at

> In Spanish, John 11:35 is still the shortest verse: "Jesús lloró" (Nueva Versión Internacional).

that point they probably just call it "supper.") Jesus predicts they'll all be ditching him soon, especially Judas, who might as well have BETRAYER silk-screened onto his robe. Judas splits. Jesus and the remaining Eleven retire to the Garden of Gethsemane, where he prays and they sleep. Then Judas strides in, backed by a rowdy posse, and plants a big one on the cheek of his former boss. Jesus gets arrested.

The religious leaders and teachers of the Law put him on trial that very night. Hanging around outside the festivities, Peter gets asked three times whether he knows that Christ fellow who just got picked up by the cops. Peter answers each inquiry with a concrete "nope." Cue rooster.

The next day, Pilate questions Jesus but can't find a reason to sentence him, other than the hysterical calls from the crucifixion-clamoring crowd. So he shakes off his backbone and concedes to the teeming masses. Pilate frees a known criminal named Barabbas and ships Jesus off to be scourged, beaten to a bloody heap, nailed to a chunk of wood, and crucified.

For additional details, please contact *Gibson, Mel.*

It's Friday afternoon when Jesus dies. Nearby, in the Jerusalem Temple, the curtain—a thick, lush cloth dividing the Most Holy Place from the rest of the sacred building—rips from top to bottom in a burst of effective symbolism. Jesus' followers ease him down from the cross, prepare him for burial, and seal him up in a cave tomb belonging to Joseph of Arimathea. For good measure, Pilate posts a handful of Roman soldiers nearby to keep things quiet.

> In Luther's German Bible, John 11:35 is a lot longer: "Und Jesus gingen die Augen über."

Easier said than done. A bunch of women show up at the tomb early Sunday morning and quickly notice that the big rock is, like, not there anymore. It's been rolled aside. A glowing angelic guy appears and announces that Jesus has risen from the dead. The ladies jet into town to spread the news, and suddenly Jesus materializes *right there* with them. They collapse in a heap and start to worship. Over the next few weeks, this kind of scenario happens a lot.

## ACTS

It's Jerusalem, post-resurrection, and Jesus is hanging with the apostles. He gives them a commissioning of sorts and then—*crack*—apparates up to heaven. The disciples choose Matthias to pinch-hit for Judas, who by this time has killed himself. On the day of Pentecost, all the Christians are still buzzing about this resurrection thing and worshiping together when a rip-roaring gust of the Holy Spirit starts flapping robes and making everyone chatter in different languages. Peter steps up to preach, and a major revival breaks out. Energized, Peter and John start going around healing folks, preaching about Jesus, and generally riling up the religious authorities. Same goes for a guy named Stephen, who gets stoned to death for talking too fervently about his resurrected Savior. A noted Pharisee named Saul serves as coat-check boy for Stephen's official stoners. A few chapters later, this same Saul gets spotlighted—and temporarily blinded—by Jesus himself on the road to Damascus:

> **Authoritative voice from out of the light:** "Saul? It's me, Jesus. Quit it with all the persecuting."
> **Saul:** "Done."

Saul changes his name to Paul and becomes the face of the early Church. He starts planting new congregations and encouraging Christians like a circuit-riding theological colossus. He gets tossed in jail, whipped, beaten, and shipwrecked, but keeps truckin' with the Gospel. He preaches wherever he can. He offends the Roman authorities. Acts closes with Paul under house arrest in Rome, which gives him plenty of time to write letters. Including ...

## ROMANS

Paul's letter to believers in Rome, a complex epistle that outlines the meat of Christian doctrine in just a few short theology-packed chapters. This is Paul's longest letter, and the crux of his argument is that following the Law is powerless when it comes to salvation. No human is righteous, which sucks. And which also means we can't save ourselves. The only source of salvation? The only rescue from the dregs of sin? The only hope for fallen humanity? It's faith in Jesus Christ.

# 1 & 2 CORINTHIANS

The church at Corinth has big problems. The city itself is
this ancient mash-up of the Vegas Strip, Bourbon Street, and
Amsterdam's red-light district all rolled into one saucy burrito.
Same goes for its church. In the first letter, Paul jumps head-on
into the mess, warning his readers about congregational divisions,
lawsuits, chaotic worship services, marriage and divorce, and even
sex scandals (according to rumor, one believer is knockin' boots
with his stepmother[4]). All kinds of unique-to-their-situation stuff,
with the famous "love chapter" appearing right in the middle.

In the second letter, Paul talks about himself. Apparently those
Corinthian wackos paid *some* attention—just a little—to his
challenges in the first letter, but something else has gone wrong:
someone's called Paul's authority into question. Crap. So Paul
spends a good chunk of 2 Corinthians defending himself and
his ministry. He outlines his credentials and owns up to his own
limitations (including the mysterious "thorn" in his flesh, from 2
Corinthians 12:7). Then he encourages the Corinthian church—a
*Gentile* church, mind you—to participate in a fundraising campaign
for poor, Jewish famine victims in Jerusalem. Ecumenism rocks.

# GALATIANS

A crew of Jewish Christians roll into Galatia and start demanding
that believers pull down their trousers and join the Snippy Brigade.
Yep, circumcision. And they need to do other Jewishy stuff, too,
like stick to the kosher guidelines. Paul jumps all over these legalists
and tells how he and Peter just had a knock-down, drag-out
argument about the same thing. Salvation doesn't come through
the outward stuff you do, Paul tells them. It's by faith, not works.
Grace, not karma. He tells them to get hooked on the freedom to

do good and live by the Spirit.[5] It's not about the rules—at least not anymore, God bless the book of Leviticus—but about becoming a new person in Christ.

## EPHESIANS

Ephesus is a big town and sort of a spiritual hub for a bunch of different churches. Since this letter from Paul probably gets passed around from church to church, Paul packs it full of his favorite themes. He hits on the bigness of God's love, the importance of unity, and the need for believers to submit to each other out of reverence for Christ's ultimate submission on the cross. Paul also tells slaves to obey their earthly masters with "respect and fear," just like they might obey the Lord. But we'll forgive him for that.[6]

## PHILIPPIANS

A joyful book, which is odd considering that the shackles on Paul's wrists probably muck up his handwriting as he composes it. According to tradition, Paul writes his letter to the church in Philippi while under house arrest in Rome—just about the time the Roman emperor Nero starts slathering Christians in tar and lighting them as torches for his banquets. Bad dude, that Nero. Anyway, Paul advises his readers to rejoice despite being set on fire or being otherwise exposed to misfortune. Embrace humility. Don't complain. Don't worry. Be like me—I'm clanking my chains together and singing a jaunty tune! Why? Because Christ suffered, and in suffering, we become more like him.

Which is why those God-wants-you-to-be-rich-and-happy televangelists don't preach very often from Philippians.

---

5. We get the famous "fruit of the Spirit" passage in Galatians 5:22–23.
6. Ephesians 6:5. To Paul's credit, he tells slave owners to treat their slaves with respect. A nice thought, but wouldn't truly respectful treatment involve, you know, *not* owning them as slaves? Paul himself points out in Colossians that, in Christ, there's no distinction between "slave or free" (Col. 3:11).

## COLOSSIANS

Another prison letter, this one to the church in Colossae, where believers are being fleeced by some ludicrous variations on the Gospel, including angel worship. Paul preaches the freedom of Christians over "the written code" (see ya, Mosaic Law!) and the power of Christ over sin. He caps it off with a few rules for holy living (put to death your sexual immorality, lust, and greed ... not to mention your angel worship) and encourages Christians to clothe themselves with kindness and compassion.[7] In fact, just clothe yourselves, *period*. It helps curtail that sexual immorality thing.

## 1 & 2 THESSALONIANS

*Letter 1*:

Dear church at Thessalonica ...

A bunch of you have been asking me questions about when Jesus will return. I'm not exactly privy to that kind of info, but let's live like it could be tomorrow. When it does happen? It'll go down in a snap. We'll hear the voice of the archangel and some heavenly trumpets, and we'll be snatched up to heaven in the rapture.[8] It'll be great. Someone should write a best-selling series of apocalyptic thrillers about this event.

Grace and peace, Paul

*Letter 2*:

Okay, people—some of you are taking this Left Behind thing a little too seriously. I've heard there's a memo floating around that supposedly says the rapture's already happened and the day of the Lord has passed us by. Are you kidding me? Relax, Thessalonians. Get back to work. You didn't miss the bus. Stop sitting around

7. These examples come from Colossians 3.
8. 1 Thessalonians 4:16–17

waiting for the Apocalypse to come knocking. You'll know it when it gets here.

Grace and peace, Paul

## 1 & 2 TIMOTHY

Paul's young missionary friend, Timothy, ends up in a leadership/teaching position in Ephesus. Kid's pretty young to be leading a church, so in the first letter, Paul gives Timothy specific advice about how to keep a church operating smoothly. For instance, you don't want a bunch of lying drunks as your deacons, so choose men worthy of respect. Also, make sure church members take care of the widows in your community. Oh, and one more thing: don't allow any women to hold positions of authority, because ladies ought to be silent in church. Huh. Two out of three ain't bad.

The next letter to Timothy continues the thread. More instructions about pastoring, with a little more emotion thrown in— Paul's writing it while locked up in Rome, and he seems ready to pass the torch. He knows death is near.

> "Most people are bothered by those passages of Scripture they do not understand, but the passages that bother me are those I do understand."
> —Mark Twain
> (1835–1910)

He also knows Timothy is well-suited to pick up where he leaves off, so he tells him to keep the faith, fight the good fight, and get ready for a little suffering.

## TITUS

Another how-to-run-a-church letter. This one's written by Paul to Titus, a guy sent to lead the church in Crete. More warnings about the dangers of those Christians who think the faith needs to be a big, exclusive, circumsized-only club. Plus, advice on what should be taught to various groups—old men, old women, young men, young women, and even slaves.[9] He closes with a quick reminder that salvation is through grace—it's a free gift that can't be earned—which is a theme dear to Paul's heart and at the core of Christian theology.

## PHILEMON

More than any of Paul's letters, this is a personal one. And it's about a personal problem. Paul gets to know a runaway slave named Onesimus, who has jumped the fence at Philemon's plantation and is hiding out when Paul converts him. Paul convinces Onesimus to return to his master with this letter in tow. In it, Paul encourages Philemon, a leader of the Colossian church, to accept his slave back as a brother in Christ—not a runaway slave. You should welcome Onesimus, Paul tells Philemon, just like you would welcome *me*. Which is a completely revolutionary thought. Because in these days Philemon has every right to execute the law-breaking Onesimus on the spot. Gulp.

## HEBREWS

Now that we're done reading Paul's mail, let's rip open a few more letters from other writers. First up is Anonymous, author of Hebrews.[10] This guy's got the Old Testament on the brain, trying to encourage believers who are just about ready to trade in their

9. Uncomfortable with Paul's seeming acceptance of slavery? Join the club. It should be noted, however, that back in biblical times, society saw nothing wrong with owning slaves. It was a lot like the early nineteenth century in America, when anyone who could afford a slave probably had one.

10. For a long time, folks assumed that Paul wrote Hebrews. It's crammed full of theology, for one thing, which is why even luminaries like Saint Augustine thought Paul wrote it. But the author never identifies himself like Paul does in every one of his other letters, nor does he address it to any specific church or person. Therefore most modern scholars doubt Paul's authorship.

new, exciting, torture-rific Christian faith for the more traditional and much less persecuted Jewish religion. Drawing heavily on OT Scripture and references to the Torah, the author builds a point-by-point case for why Christianity beats Judaism any day. Sure, it's a risky way to believe, he says. But the payoff's worth it.

## JAMES

Martin Luther *hated* this book, traditionally written by one of Jesus' younger brothers.[11] Why? Because Luther was intoxicated with Paul's message of salvation by faith alone, and James goes on and on about the importance of good works. Faith without works, James says, is no faith at all. He argues that a truly authentic faith will bleed over into the way a person lives—particularly in one's concern for the poor.[12]

## 1 & 2 PETER

Simon Peter—the foremost of Jesus' disciples and a major leader of the early Church—tries his hand at letter writing. In the first one, he addresses Christians in Asia Minor who are being persecuted for their faith. He tells them to buck up and remember that Jesus endured his share of persecution back in the day. Suffering for the sake of Christ is a *privilege*, so quit whining.

In the second letter, he rails against false teachers and tells his readers to always be ready for the end of the world. To look forward to it, even, because it's the "day of the Lord."[13] Sure, the global destruction won't be much fun, but the resulting new heaven and new earth will be sweet.

One of the coolest parts of the second letter is that Peter actually mentions Paul's writings in chapter 3. According to Peter, Paul's

11. For more details about Luther's feelings toward James and a handful of other New Testament books, skip ahead to page 145 in the next chapter.
12. James 5:1–6 lays down the smack *hard* on "rich oppressors" who hoard wealth at the expense of the working class. Wealthy, white evangelical Republicans going around begging for tax cuts would have made his eyes bleed.
13. 2 Peter 3:10

letters contain "some things that are hard to understand" (2 Pet. 3:16). Man. If Saint Peter has trouble figuring this stuff out, the *Pocket Guide*'s got problems.

## I, 2, & 3 JOHN

Letters from the author of the Gospel of John. In Letter 1, he immediately gets in a scrape with Gnosticism, a growing cult that denies Jesus was ever a man. (These Gnostics think anything physical—like a person's body—is flat-out evil. A holy God could never wrap himself up in such filth. So they decide that the Jesus who walked around with the disciples and healed people was a phantom. *Wooooo.*) Anyway, John thinks this is garbage, because he spent years actually backpacking through the Palestinian countryside with the (alleged) Phantom Son of God. So he warns his readers not to get caught up in that sort of philosophical nuttiness.

In the second letter, John writes to a mysterious "chosen lady and her children." Is it a figure of speech referring to a nearby church and its members? A note to a particular mom and her kids? A *Brady Bunch* allusion? No one knows. What we do know is that it's the shortest book in the Bible, with only thirteen verses. Half of them are about loving one another. The other half are about avoiding false teachers.

Letter 3 goes out to Gaius, one of John's buddies. It's short, too. In it, John calls out some church guy named Diotrephes, who's being an arrogant, gossipy, inhospitable knucklehead. John promises to deal with him "face to face." Yep, John's ready to chew gum and bust some teeth, and ... gum hasn't been invented yet.

## JUDE

Barely three verses into this tiny twenty-five-verse book, Jude tells us how disappointed he is. He wants to write something really catchy and inspiring about salvation, but unfortunately there are some false teachers causing trouble in the church. These scoffers are particularly bad, as they keep denying the deity of Christ and treating their bodies like amusement parks. Too bad for them, Jude says, because they'll suffer some Old Testament-style smiting.

Interestingly, Jude quotes from two non-canonical sources: The Assumption of Moses (verse 9, a reference to the archangel Michael's battle with the devil about the body of Moses) and the book of Enoch (verse 14). Skating a little close to the edge there, Jude.

## REVELATION

The last and most controversial book in the Bible. It's "the revelation of Jesus Christ" (verse 1) to John, zapped into the elderly apostle's brain while in exile on the isle of Patmos. And like any vision, it's a bit ... loopy. And intimidating. And a little scary, if lion-toothed, human-faced, scorpion-tailed locust assassins give you the heebie-jeebies.

After seeing someone "like a son of man" hanging around a bunch of lampstands (1:13)—it turns out to be Jesus, who wants John to write down what he's about to see—John kicks off the freakiness with some harsh statements to several local churches. Then he glimpses a throne in heaven, surrounded by four living creatures covered with eyes. And wings. Then a bloodied, already-slain lamb, perched in the center of the throne, starts breaking seals. (No, not the sleek, whiskered arctic creatures, mind you ... we're talking the kind of wax seals that keep parchment closed. Jesus wouldn't hurt cute baby seals.)

These seals unleash all kinds of chaos and destruction, including (but not limited to) the Four Horsemen of the Apocalypse, a terrible earthquake, a blood-red moon, and stars falling from the sky. Then it's quiet for a half-hour, until seven angels show up and start blowing their trumpets. With every horn blast comes more chaos and destruction. Hail mixed with blood starts dropping to the earth, wreaking havoc with local insurance agencies. A third of the sea turns to blood. A meteorite/comet/star falls to earth, poisoning a third of the water. The sixth trumpet looses four angels leading 200 million mounted troops who are instructed to kill a third of mankind. Pretty bad stuff.

> "The New Testament is the very best book that ever was or ever will be known in the world."
> —Charles Dickens
> (1812–1870)

Two "witnesses" hit the scene and start prophesying and breathing fire on people who dispute them. No, really: fire-breathing. Then the witnesses die. Then they come back to life and freak everyone out. A pregnant woman and a dragon (ye olde Lucifer) drop down from heaven. The dragon tries to eat the woman's baby, dingo-style, until a big heavenly battle breaks out. The dragon falls to earth, where he's met by a beast rising out of the sea. Lookee! It's the Antichrist! He performs all these miraculous signs and deceives everyone on earth into worshiping him. These gullible worshipers end up receiving the "mark of the beast" (13:16). Which is bad.

Before long, seven angels start tipping out bowls of God's wrath. Those sporting the mark of the beast get boils. The sea turns to blood. The sun burns so hot, people start to catch fire. The earth is plunged into darkness. The Euphrates River dries up—which is *so* inconvenient, because how else are the people on fire gonna put themselves out?

But it ain't over yet. The Whore of Babylon rides into town on the back of a bright-red, seven-headed creature covered with filthy graffiti. Then Jesus gallops in on a white horse—with "eyes like blazing fire," followed by the armies of heaven (19:12–14)—to wage war on the beast and its rider. Waging commences. The beast is defeated and thrown into the lake of fire. Satan is bound for a thousand years and locked up in the Abyss. There is much debate among Christians about how to interpret this thousand-year stuff,[14] but when it's over, Satan gets a new home in the lake of fire, where he'll be tormented forever and ever. Yay! The dead are judged according to what they've done.

"Behold," a voice from the throne says, "I make all things new."[15] And a glistening, renovated Jerusalem descends from heaven. It's a wonderful place, with no death, no crying, no pain. It's lit by the glory of God, and everything that got screwed up in the Garden of Eden gets made right. And it'll be right forever and ever.

The vision ends. John takes a deep breath, then wraps the Bible up with a quick, powerful, three-word prayer: "Come, Lord Jesus."

Amen.

14. These beliefs are discussed in fascinating detail in *Pocket Guide to the Apocalypse: The Official Field Manual for the End of the World* (RELEVANT Books, 2005), written—surprisingly enough—by this very author. It's a lot like this book, except the whole thing is about the book of Revelation.
15. Revelation 21:5, KJV

**06**

# THE BRIEF HISTORY
# OF HOLY WRIT
## (A TIMELINE)

ontrary to the Bible-thumping assumptions of a few
brands of fundamentalist evangelicalism, the Good Book
didn't just fall from heaven one day, bound in black
leather, assembled into chapters and verses, and translated
into English by a certain King James with the words of Christ
helpfully highlighted in red. The Bible started as a bunch of ancient
documents—or in some cases, scraps of documents—written and
copied by ancient scribes. The journey from dusty papyrus to
gold-lined onionskin is a long one. The process includes a lot of
translating, arguing about translating, killing people because of their
translating, and revising the translating.

Here, then, is the blood-soaked road from the first draft of
Genesis to the much-ballyhooed King James Version of the Bible.

# 900-ISH BC

**Someone writes, transcribes, or otherwise assembles the Pentateuch.**

It might have been Moses who did it. He's the star of the stories, for one thing, and both Jewish and Christian tradition have always credited him with the authorship and/or editing of the Pentateuch. Besides, we call Genesis, Exodus, Leviticus, Numbers, and Deuteronomy the "Books of Moses," right?

But more recent scholarship thinks the books are more likely a documentary-style compilation of stories from ancient sources, the result of years and years of editing and recording by a motley collection of priestly scribes. At any rate, the "writing" of the Pentateuch comes to pass a thousand years or so before Jesus shows up. It puts decades of oral tradition into written form. It outlines the basic structure of Israel's faith. And it introduces us to epic figures like Noah, Abraham, and Joseph. Not to mention less epic figures like Shepho, son of Shobal.[1]

# 400 BC

**Malachi, the last book of the Old Testament, is written.**

The OT goes out with a bang, warning Israel of impending judgment in a short little book brought to us by a minor prophet named Malachi. At least, we *think* his name is Malachi. No one really knows. Verse 1 tells us up front that what we're getting is "the word of the Lord to Israel through Malachi." Which is a fairly straightforward way of identifying one's authorship, until we find out that in Hebrew, *Malachi* means "my messenger." Hmm. Maybe Malachi isn't really a name. Maybe it's a title—or, at least, a chest-thumping nickname. Since the book itself skimps on any other info about "Malachi" and his role as holy mouthpiece, the prophet's true identity remains a mystery. Might have been one of Ezra's assistants, as some theories suggest. Could have been Shepho, son of Shobal, for all we know. People lose sleep over this kind of thing.

## 300–200 BC

### Ptolemy Philadelphus commissions the Septuagint.

Legend has it that the Egyptian pharaoh Ptolemy Philadelphus wants his own private translation of the Torah to display in the library in Alexandria, right up front near the magazines. And what Philly wants, Philly gets, so seventy-two Jewish scholars—six scribes from each of the twelve tribes of Israel—are commissioned to translate the Hebrew Old Testament into Greek. The translators sequester themselves into separate chambers, and lo and behold, the whole bunch of them produce identical versions of the holy text in precisely seventy-two days. Shazam! This super-spiritual history comes our way courtesy of generally reliable folks like Josephus, Philo of Alexandria, and Tertullian, who get their info from an ancient document called the Letter of Aristeas. But most modern scholars think everyone's a little too zealous about the whole *woo-woo* origin story—hoping, perhaps, to bulk up the translation with some divine authority.

Regardless of how it gets here, the resulting Septuagint (Latin for "seventy"; known on the street as LXX) sets the standard for the Old Testament. It contains the customary thirty-nine OT books, plus seven additional apocryphal books—documents not recognized as canonical by Protestant Christians or Orthodox Jews.[2] Nevertheless, the translation is way influential: most of

2. Also known as *pseudoepigraphal* books, but *apocryphal* is lots easier to say.

the OT references in the New Testament are quotes from the Septuagint. And most early Christian translations of the OT use the Greek Septuagint for source material, because the original ancient Hebrew—what with its crazy lack of vowels and everything—is just *hard*, you know?

---

## AD 90

---

### The Council of Jamnia establishes the Jewish canon.

A bunch of rabbinical scholars huddle up after the fall of Jerusalem in AD 70 and literally spend years discussing the canonical status of several Old Testament books. Tradition states the huddle is quarterbacked by a Jewish hero named Yohanan ben Zakkai, a descendant of the house of David.[3] The Yohanan-led rabbis are said to have decided the seven apocryphal books of the Septuagint weren't quite Bible-worthy. And that's that. They close the book, so to speak, on the thirty-nine books of the Old Testament canon.

---

## AD 100-ISH

---

### Last books in the New Testament written. Probably.

See, no one's really certain when the last canonical New Testament book gets penned, or even which books should be dated last. It's not like Paul's a slave to the rules of modern letter composition, opening each epistle with a crisp "May 5, AD 43. Dear Church at Ephesus ..." Still, tradition holds that Paul's letters are the earliest written documents of the New Testament. The Gospels of Matthew and Mark probably appear next, somewhere past the mid-century point. Luke writes his Gospel and the book of

---

3. Tradition also states that Yohanan ben Zakkai escaped the siege of Jerusalem by being ferried to safety in a coffin. Which scores high on creativity points, but bravery? Not so much.

Acts a few years later. Most agree that John's additions to the canon are among the final NT documents to be written. His Gospel and the book of Revelation, according to most conservative scholars, show up toward the end of the century.

That's the good news.

The bad news is that every single one of these apparent "facts" is in dispute somewhere, by any number of well-reasoned,

> Apparently, there's a Bible at the University of Gottingen, Germany, that's written on 2,470 palm leaves. The reason for its existence is unclear.

Greek-reading eggheads. Some speculate the writing of the entire New Testament wraps up by AD 70, the year invading Roman armies destroy the Temple in Jerusalem.[4] Others place Paul's letters no earlier than AD 49–51.

At any rate, by the year AD 120, leading Christians like Polycarp are referencing as many as sixteen of the books that will eventually be canonized as parts of the New Testament.[5]

---

## AD 150

---

**Wealthy ship owner Marcion first proposes an exclusive canon.**

But Marcion's a full-fledged heretic, so his list hardly counts. He completely rejects the violent, eye-for-an-eye Old Testament, on account of how it seems seriously incompatible with the lovey-dovey teachings of Jesus. In fact, Marcion suggests the cruel, capricious, law-giving deity of the OT is an entirely separate cosmic ruler from the "Supreme God of Love" as revealed by

---

4. Here's why: both Matthew and Luke record Jesus prophesying about the eventual destruction of the Temple in Jerusalem. Weird, isn't it, that none of them throw in any sort of smug aside that says, "By the way, this prophecy came true in AD 70. Snap!" Because that's what the *Pocket Guide* would do. For this reason, a handful of evangelical scholars believe the canon was completed prior to the Temple's destruction.
5. This occurs in Polycarp's letter to the church at Phillipi. It's a *long* letter.

Christ.[6] So Marcion's Bible is OT-free. Most of the Gospels don't make the cut either, as they're way too friendly toward Judaism.

According to Marcion's build-your-own-Bible philosophy, the only true Scriptures are ten of Paul's letters and a few highly edited selections from the Gospel of Luke.

Though his beliefs gain minor footholds among anti-Semites, most Christians conclude that Marcion's a turd. (His own family doesn't even like him much. His father, a bishop, excommunicates him for immorality.) But Marcion's cloudy thinking comes with a silver lining: as great a challenge as his theories pose to early Christian doctrine, they at least make everyone aware of the importance of figuring out which texts are (and aren't) canonical.

> "The existence of the Bible, as a book for the people, is the greatest benefit which the human race has ever experienced. Every attempt to belittle it is a crime against humanity."
> —Immanuel Kant
> (1724–1804)

## AD 367

**Athanasius lists the New Testament canon.**

In nothing less than his annual Easter letter, Saint Athanasius, bishop of Alexandria, provides a handy list of the New Testament books he considers to be canonical. This is the first list that directly matches the modern-day New Testament. It's not exactly unanimous, though; a few of the entries in the "inspired" column continue to be disputed among early Church leaders. These divisive books include Hebrews (no one can figure out who wrote it),

Jude (quotes shamelessly from the apocryphal book of Enoch), and Revelation (too easily appropriated by apocalyptic nutjobs). Regardless, many Protestants give props to Athanasius as the father of the New Testament canon.

## AD 382

**Jerome busts out the Vulgate.**

In a lovely burst of populism, Pope Damasus decides the Church needs an official translation of the Bible that's accessible to the common folk, who speak Latin. So he enlists his official secretary, a razor-tongued scholar and monk named Eusebius Hieronymus Sophronius—called Jerome by his friends, thank God—to produce the first true translation of the entire Bible. Twenty-three years later, Jerome completes the Vulgate, possibly the most influential Scripture translation in history and definitely the one with the dirtiest-sounding name. Christians use this translation for the next thousand years. It's directly responsible for Latin becoming the de facto language of Western Christianity. In fact, the Vulgate is responsible for the *Pocket Guide*'s use of *de facto* in the previous sentence. Thanks, Jerome!

## AD 397

**Third Synod of Carthage approves the present New Testament canon.**

Or, more accurately, they ratify the canonical list accepted by the Synod of Hippo Regius in AD 393, which has nothing to do with hippopotami and everything to do with an ancient North African city in present-day Algeria. Another official council in Carthage in

AD 419 gives a thumbs-up to the same list. And thus the biblical canon goes into lockdown.

---

## AD 600

---

### A long period of not-much-happening kicks off.

Welcome to the Middle Ages. Bible-wise, all's quiet in Western Europe. This interlude between the end of classical culture (around the fifth century) and the onset of medieval culture (eleventh century) generally sees a lot of ... well, no one's too sure. Marauding hordes? Grubby pagans? Thatched huts? It's a virtual news blackout, which is why the era is commonly known as the "Dark Ages." Hardly any written record, as few people could write. Not much reading, either. The only Good Book around is Jerome's Vulgate, and by this time, only priests have the educational wherewithal to read Latin. Everyone else? Pretty much just has to take their word for it.

---

## AD 800

---

### Celtic monks produce the Book of Kells.

Despite the relative silence of Middle-Aged Europe, Christianity flourishes in Ireland, thanks to legendary missionary figures like Saint Patrick and Saint Columba. At some point during this period—most experts now peg it around AD 800—monks create the extraordinary Book of Kells at the famed island monastery of Iona, off the western coast of Scotland. An elaborately illustrated Latin manuscript of the four gospels, The Book of Kells is considered one of the finest specimens of Irish writing and craftsmanship in existence. In fact, many historians believe the document to be one of the most significant works of art to survive the entire medieval period. It's safe to say more people would be into the Bible if all of them looked as magically delicious as this one.

---

## 1205[7]

**The Bible gets chapter-and-versified.**

Up to this point, the Old and New Testaments are just a whole bunch of long, divinely inspired documents containing history, prose, poetry, begats, moral instructions, and the occasional apocalyptic scenario. Words and sentences piled upon words and sentences. Then Stephen Langton, Archbishop of Canterbury, comes along. And with the enthusiasm of an obsessive-compulsive librarian, he oversees the production of an edition of the Vulgate with all those rambling books divided into chapter and verse. Genius! With slight modification, today's Bibles still follow his arrangement. Which means we owe well-known verses like John 3:16 not so much to the Gospel writers but to this guy.

---

## 1380

**Wycliffe applies a little English to Scripture.**

Thanks to Oxford professor and philosopher John Wycliffe—a reformer who hates monasteries, distrusts monks, and wears his frustration with the institutional tendencies of the Roman Catholic Church right there on his, uh, robey sleeve thing—the Bible makes the significant leap from stuffy Latin to common English. Back in the fourteenth century, everyone's still carrying around frayed copies of Jerome's Vulgate, though the only people who can actually read the thing are scholars and clergy. Wycliffe thinks this is bunk. (He thinks a lot of things are bunk.) So he gathers up a

---

7. At this point, the *Pocket Guide*'s gonna drop the AD designation. Welcome, everyone, to the Common Era.

bunch of disciples and sets them loose on a fun project: producing dozens of hand-written copies of the Bible in the English language, translated out of the Vulgate.[8]

Church leaders are none too pleased about this unauthorized idea and set out to destroy every Wycliffe Bible they can find. They eventually go medieval on Wycliffe, too, but not until after he dies in 1384. First they declare him a heretic. (Being dead already, this grave pronouncement is of little concern to Mr. Wycliffe.) Then, Pope Martin V orders his lackeys to dig up Wycliffe's long-dead body, crush his apostate bones into a fine powder, incinerate the leftovers, and unceremoniously toss the ashes into a river. Because that'll show him who's boss! (Or, at least, who's being all weird about his Latin!)

> For $2.75 million at *www. greatsite.com* ("World's Largest Dealer of Rare and Antique Bibles"), you can buy a hand-written copy of a Wycliffe Bible dating back to 1410. It's missing the title page to 1 Thessalonians, though, so there's some room to haggle.

**Postscript:** Tradition credits Wycliffe with leading the Church out of the Dark Ages by getting the Word of God back into the hands of the people. Despite the Great English Bible Roundup of the 1300s, the Wycliffe Bible ends up being widely distributed throughout England. Kinda like old dead Mr. Wycliffe himself.

---

## 1411

### Reformer Jan Hus executed for supporting Wycliffe's Bible.

And not just executed, but burned at the stake with copies of

---

8. There's dispute as to whether Wycliffe actually did any of the translating himself, as Church tradition has long believed. Most likely, he played more of a cheerleading role—*great job with that conjugation, fellas!*—inspiring the project and leading it to completion.

Wycliffe's work used as kindling. Or so the story goes. Don't let all that "love one another" crap fool you. If there's one thing the medieval Church will absolutely not tolerate, it's people reading the Bible for themselves.

## 1456

**Gutenberg shuffles type, changes world.**

A mysterious young German blessed with innovative thinking and a trunkload of money-making schemes, Johann Gutenberg figures out that metal typography is more efficient than the hand-carved wood-block technique popular at the time. So he designs his own printing system with moveable type and starts mass-producing the Latin Vulgate translation. Gutenberg presses out something like 180 copies, a handful of which still exist.[9]

Churches and monasteries go crazy over it, because this means they don't have to sit around for twenty years while some nearsighted monk toils over a hand-copied edition of Scripture, fighting the twin demons of carpal tunnel syndrome and smudged calligraphy. Also, the thing's in Latin—not common vernacular English or German—so they can get behind this baby for sure.

Gutenberg hardly makes any money from his Bibles (he's tons more successful printing indulgences for the Catholic Church), but his invention pretty much changes the world.[10] The printing press gives rise to the publishing industry, books flood the market, literacy spreads like the plague, and before long, Europe's basking in the Renaissance.

9. In the United States, you can see one at the following locations: the Library of Congress, the New York Public Library, NYC's Pierpont Morgan Library, Yale University, Harvard University, Princeton University, Indiana University, the University of Texas at Austin, the Huntington Library in San Marino, California, and on James Dobson's coffee table. Just kidding about the Dobson part.
10. For instance, more books were printed between 1460 and 1500 than had been transcribed by monks and scribes during the entire Middle Ages.

## 1516

**Erasmus shoves Jerome aside with a new Latin translation.**

Why? He's a brilliant Greek scholar, for one thing, and one who suspects Jerome's Vulgate translation from Greek to Latin to be woefully inadequate. And Erasmus is not the kind of guy who just sits around complaining about inadequacies, all whine and no action. This is a guy, after all, who's born illegitimately with the goofy Dutch name Gerrit Gerritszoon (English equivalent: Pete Peterson). Knowing this exponentially increases his wedgie potential, he scraps the lame name as soon as he's able, assuming a fancy-pants Greek moniker instead: Erasmus. Dude gets things done.

Back to the Bible. Erasmus never gets too jazzed by the Vulgate, so he does what any other theological luminary would do: he produces a brand-new Latin translation of his own. He prints the Latin side by side with the original Greek, and his parallel New Testament is a major hit. It's got several things going for it, not the least of which is that it's the first fresh Latin translation of the Bible in more than a thousand years. Also, it's printed in sweet moveable type. The Erasmus NT earns the nickname *Textus Receptus* ("received text"), and later becomes the underlying basis for the King James translation of the Bible. Dorky little Pete Peterson makes it big.

## 1525–1526

**William Tyndale translates and prints the Bible into common English.**

Wycliffe may have scored first by translating Scripture into

English, but his elegant handwritten manuscripts are *so* fourteenth century. Tyndale is hip to the technology of his day and takes full advantage of Gutenberg's printing press. A scholar said to have been fluent in eight languages, Tyndale and his Bible hit big. He's frequently pegged as the "architect of the English language" and makes the impressive moniker stick—he introduces all kinds of new words and phrases into the mother tongue, translated from the original Greek and Hebrew.

*Scapegoat*, *atonement*, *Passover*, *brother's keeper*, and *the powers that be* are ours, courtesy of Mr. Tyndale.

It's not all cupcakes and butterflies, though. These "powers that be" aren't exactly throwing Tyndale a parade for his contributions to sixteenth-century religious life. They get wind of his common-language New Testament and ban it midway through the first printing in 1525, forcing him to finish the process in secret a year later.[11] His printed pages get distributed anyway, smuggled into England in bales of hay and cloth. Any copies discovered by the Church get torched. Tyndale makes the most-wanted list and heads for the hills. Eleven years later, he's captured, arrested, strangled, and burned at the stake—apparently in that order.

> "Another century and there will not be a Bible on earth!"
> —Voltaire
> (1694–1778)

---

## 1534

**Martin Luther publishes the full Bible in common German.**

Luther, the German theologian and monk whose teaching

---

11. He never finishes printing and translating the whole Bible, as being on the run for a decade tends to cause significant delays in production. Tyndale's English translations include the New Testament, the Pentateuch, and the books of Joshua, Judges, Ruth, 1 & 2 Samuel, 1 & 2 Kings, 1 & 2 Chronicles, and Jonah.

inspires the Protestant Reformation, wants—like Wycliffe and Tyndale—to get the Bible into the hands of the common folk and, as a nice byproduct, give the powerful church authorities a good poke in the eye. So he translates the Good Book into German. Along the way, however, Luther can't resist taking a few jabs at the Bible itself. He's unimpressed by eternally controversial books like Jude, James, Hebrews, and especially Revelation (a book he can't even *fathom* as having been inspired by the Holy Spirit). Still, he begrudgingly includes these four books in his translation ... but he sticks them at the end, rather than in the traditional New Testament order.[12] Other parts of the Bible aren't so lucky. Luther ditches the apocryphal books of the Old Testament, because even though they show up in the Greek Septuagint, the Hebrew Scriptures don't claim them.[13] And for the Council of Jamnia's sake, wouldn't the Jews know what's what in the OT? Verily, Protestants follow Luther's lead. Which means today's Protestant Bibles, almost five hundred years later, are still apocrypha-free. Uncle Marty would be proud.

> "I am going to put the Bible out of business."
> —Robert Ingersoll
> (1833–1899)

---

## 1535

---

**Portions of the Church-approved Coverdale Bible hit the street.**

Another incomplete Bible gets translated into English, but

---

12. German-language Luther Bibles *still* put these four books at the end of the New Testament. Then again, Revelation is always at the end, so that's only three-quarters remarkable.

13. He thinks they're good reading and everything, and spiritually beneficial. But books like 2 Maccabees just don't set his "divinely inspired" radar to buzzing. Probably because they tend to emphasize Catholic doctrines like purgatory and prayer for the dead.

there's no hay-bale-hiding required on this one. It comes from the well-studied mind of Miles Coverdale, an ordained priest and Augustinian friar. Serious Catholic cred. Miles is a former assistant of Tyndale, but unlike his ex-boss, he gets ecclesiastic approval for his translation. It comes off the presses with a flattering dedication to Henry VIII—the married-six-times king of England—and a few of his translations of the Psalms are still in use today by the Church of England.

## 1536

**John Rogers assembles the first complete English Bible out of Tyndale and Coverdale scraps.**

A friend of William Tyndale, John Rogers combines Coverdale's Old Testament stuff with Tyndale's NT and Pentateuch to form what's generally referred to as Matthew's Bible. (Thanks to a fair amount of translator persecution in the news, Rogers chooses to publish it under the pseudonym Thomas Matthew. He gets his fake name on the cover primarily for adding some prefaces and margin notes, not because he plays any sort of role in the translating process.) The king licenses a few copies and legally sells it in England. A few years later, Rogers gets the Reformation bug and starts speaking out against the Church of Rome, disrespecting the pope, and denying the real presence of the Eucharist. Oops. All that Protestant yammering gets him burned at the stake in 1555. Might as well have put his real name on the Bible after all.

## 1539

**Henry VIII orders up the first Authorized Translation.**

The king wants a Bible to be read aloud in worship services in every church in England. He ends up with the so-called Great Bible, published by Edward Whitchurch. The translation's "great"-ness comes from the fact that, at fourteen inches high, the thing's humongous. Seriously coffee-table-sized. This Bible is another duet by the Two 'Dales, with Tyndale posthumously providing the NT and Pentateuch (translated from the original Greek and Hebrew), and Coverdale backing him up with the rest (probably translated from non-original sources like the Vulgate and Luther's German Bible). Eventually, Whitchurch is imprisoned for being a Protestant, but he gets out after a few weeks and dies in 1561 of natural causes. As opposed to, you know, fire-related ones.

---

## 1546

---

**The Council of Trent affirms the authority of the Vulgate.**

What with Luther running around nailing up theses, Erasmus criticizing the Vulgate, and Tyndale introducing "powers that be" to the local vocabulary, the Catholic Church is under tremendous pressure. So the bishops rally together for a major response: the nearly two-decades-long Council of Trent. Here, in several sessions, Church authorities hammer out the doctrines that set Catholicism apart from the burgeoning faith of the Reformers. These doctrines include the equal validity of Scripture and Tradition as sources of religious truth, the exclusive right of the Church to interpret the Bible, and—in a swipe at Luther and the Reformed Brigade—the authority of the text of Jerome's Vulgate. Which means all those apocryphal books Luther thinks are rubbish make the canonical cut. At least, the Catholic one. Scholars widely consider the Council of Trent one of the most important doctrinal councils in the history of the Catholic Church.

## 1560

**Here comes the Geneva Bible.**

The Geneva Bible is awesome. Published by exiled Protestant scholars hiding out in John Calvin's Geneva, Switzerland, this complete Bible is mostly translated from the original languages but owes a lot to Tyndale and Coverdale. Puritans become the translation's biggest fans due to its super-Calvinist Protestant flavor: it's the first English version to scrap the Apocrypha, and it comes with cross-references and helpful margin notes.[14] The Geneva Bible is likely the first English translation to hit America, crossing the Atlantic with the *Mayflower* pilgrims.

Incidentally, the Geneva Bible carries with it a rather embarrassing nickname, the "Breeches Bible"—and no, the *Pocket Guide* is not making this up—thanks to its rendition of Genesis 3:7. The verse describes how Adam and Eve, having discovered themselves to be naked, "*sewed figge tree leaues together, and made them selues breeches.*" Fig-leaf britches! Classic.

## 1568

**Seventeen authorized translators generate the Bishops' Bible.**

So the Geneva Bible, with its objectionable mega-Protestant/Calvinist stylings, is unacceptable to the bishops of the Church of England. In response, they commission yet another authorized version, led by the Archbishop of Canterbury, Matthew Parker. The language in this version is pretty stuffy, though, and the end product lacks all the reader-friendly elements—for instance, the rockin' margin notes—of the Geneva Bible. Aside from the

14. Helpful margin notes indeed. One of them proclaims the pope to be the Antichrist. Those crazy Calvinists.

bishops, few churchgoers ever get into it that much.

## 1524–1590

**Common-language Bibles get trendy across Europe.**

Translators throughout the continent, most likely sixteenth-century geeks with posters of Luther and Tyndale on their walls, get bit by the Bible bug. In 1524, the New Testament becomes available in the Schwyzerdeutsch dialect of German. A complete Dutch Bible hits shelves in 1526. A French translation of the Vulgate shows up in 1530, and Italy gets her own New Testament the same year. The Bible goes Icelandic and Swedish in 1541, Finnish in 1548, Danish in 1550, Slovene in 1557, Polish in 1561, Croat in 1563, Spanish in 1569 (a Catholic-approved translation from the Vulgate), and Hungarian in 1590. Able to read the Bible for themselves, the common folk get a lot more spiritual. The Reformation gains a lot more steam. The establishment gets a lot more worried.

## 1582

**The Roman Catholic Church comes to terms with an English translation. Finally.**

You can't hold out forever, not when practically every able-bodied theologian and his haberdasher have published their own personal common-English translations of the Bible. So a few English Catholic exiles, working in Reims, a village in northern France, set out to produce an English translation that's approved by the Church and, well, not in the business of tagging the papacy with all that Antichrist baggage. They publish their New

Testament in 1582, then move to Douai, another French locale, where they wrap up the OT in 1609. The result is the creatively identified Rheims-Douay Bible, and according to published reports, this Word of God is free from all the heretical Protestant trappings of the previous Words of God. Unfortunately, it's also considerably free from accuracy, as the translation isn't based on the original Greek and Hebrew so much as on Jerome's Latin Vulgate. Yep, a translation of a translation. And the first translation is of questionable precision to begin with. The corpse of Erasmus shudders in his grave. Meanwhile, English-speaking Roman Catholics use this version of the Bible for the next three centuries.

## 1605

### King James recruits a team to produce an authorized translation of the Bible.

Under pressure from Protestant clergy to replace the popular but sorta embarrassing Geneva Bible—and its strident Calvinism—James I of England assembles a crack team of Bible scholars. Among them are the professors of Greek and Hebrew from Oxford. A gaggle of poindexters from Cambridge also make the invitation list. James collects fifty-four scholars in all and divides them into six groups. Two teams go to Oxford, two head for Cambridge, and two set up camp in Westminster. Jimmy sends them away with explicit instructions.

> There are 592,439 words in the King James Version of the Old Testament. There would be 592,525 words if the phrase "for as much" weren't combined into the old-timey compound "forasmuch."

Number one, he says, is to follow the Bishops' Bible as closely as possible until you run into a translation problem. When this happens, consult the earlier versions too, including the Rheims Bible, the Geneva Bible (breeches!), the Coverdale Bible, the Great Bible, and Tyndale's New Testament. Get used to consulting these texts, because you're not so much charged with coming up with a new translation as developing a nice, clean revision of what we've already got.

Second, he says, get rid of all those annoying footnotes and comments cluttering up the Geneva Bible. That stuff's exhausting, so unless the text is just begging for a detailed explanation of the Greek or Hebrew, keep the margins free from your personal theology.

Third, leave in the old ecclesiastical terms (*church, baptism*) instead of going off with provocative modern translations (*community, washing*) like the Geneva Bible does. That's just asking for trouble.

And fourth, says James I of England, make sure you stick my name on this baby. It's gonna be big.[15]

James assigns each team a certain part of the Bible, and they work separately on these sections. The various drafts are then rotated around for criticism and clarification until the full crew reaches a consensus. By the time 1611 rolls around, the revisions are complete and everybody's on board. The king's authorized baby is ready to go to press.

---

## 1611

---

**The Authorized Version rolls off the presses and into history.**

Here in the United States, we call it the King James Version, but across the pond and throughout Europe, it's simply known as the

---

15. This fourth instruction of James to the translators, upon further reflection, may be apocryphal.

Authorized Version (AV). The title page indicates the long-awaited work is "appointed to be read in churches," but other than that phrase—and the fact that His Royal Highness, Jimmy the First, got the enchilada cooking in the first place—there's no formal statement of this Bible's authoritativeness.

Three editions of the AV roll out that first year, each including the Apocrypha and a couple of prefatory documents. One of these prefaces is an oozing dedication letter to King James, calling him the "principle Author and Mover of the work" and God's darkness-dispelling sunshiny gift to the worthy inhabitants of England and blah-blah-bootlicking-blah. Whatever, suck-up translators. The other preface is more valuable: a long memo from the translators to the reader, describing with great enthusiasm the necessity and value of the translation. Along the way, it can't resist taking a couple of potshots at the Catholic Church for keeping its Vulgated membership in the dark, scripturally speaking. Protestant Bible scholars *looooove* this preface, but it doesn't get printed much anymore.

What *does* get printed, at least in the first three years of the version's existence, is a slate of new editions of the AV. This is primarily because each edition has more typographical mistakes than Solomon had wives. The first AVs are littered with misprints. And each attempt to correct these holy typos seems to result in an unholy mess of new ones. Moveable type is cool and everything, but there's no *undo* command when you mislabel 1 Chronicles as 1 Corinthians (as one of the 1611 printings does). Or when you mistakenly attribute Christ's dialogue in the Garden of Gethsemane to none other than *Judas*. Gulp.

Then there's the most offensive (and/or swingin') misprint ever: a 1631 edition of the AV that conspicuously forgets the all-important *not* in Exodus 20:17. Yep, right there in the middle of the Ten Commandments. Published by Barker and Lewis, the king's printers, the resulting seventh commandment reads: "Thou shalt covet thy neighbour's wife." As a result of this gaffe, all sorts of extramarital Elizabethan-era lovin' ensues. (At least, that's the fallout as imagined by the *Pocket Guide*.) Saucy conjecture aside, the mistake earns this edition an unflattering nickname: "The Wicked Bible." It also leads to a major fine being levied against the printers. B&L go out of business and probably end up doing all kinds of coveting on account of being broke.

America's first Bible was published in 1663 in the native Algonquin language. It did okay in Quebec but never really connected in the Colonies.

Meanwhile, the importance of the King James Bible can't be overstated. Prior to the publication of the AV, a new English translation of the Bible seemed to crop up at least once a decade. Yet in the years after 1611, the only English translations printed are variations on the same Authorized Version. Some editions simply update the language and standardize spellings. Others replace the difficult-to-read black letter type with more legible Roman type. A few begin to omit the Apocrypha. But not until the late nineteenth century—when the Revised Version applies new scholarship to the field of biblical translation—do any major translations or revisions compete with King James and his Authorized Version.

The upshot is that it becomes possibly the most influential literary work ever. Its language and imagery color the writings of Bunyan, Milton, Shakespeare, Longfellow, Keats, Melville, Whitman, and just about every other luminary in the English literary canon, making it one of the principle building blocks of the English we still speak and write today. The King James Bible is important. So quit sniggering when you trip over the word "ass" every once in a while in the Old Testament.

# VERSIONS AND PERVERSIONS
## (A SELECTIVE SURVEY OF TRANSLATIONS)

ou think it's hard to distinguish between the Tyndale and Coverdale Bibles? It gets even worse. Because once biblical scholarship starts to come of age in the nineteenth century, not everyone's completely satisfied with the Scripture passed down from King James. In 1833, Noah Webster—the dictionary guy—publishes a revision to the Authorized Version, mainly to correct grammar and replace archaic words ("even-tide" becomes "evening"). He also throws in a handful of more delicate descriptions where certain KJV phrases cause his Victorian cheeks to blush ("whore" turns into "lewd woman").

In 1862, a guy named Robert Young worries that the KJV's translating policies have voided the original inspiration of Scripture, so he publishes his own Bible: Young's Literal Translation, a strictly word-for-word, original-text-to-English translation, with gobbledy results.[1]

And in 1885, the English Revised Version of the Bible hits shelves in England, for the purpose of updating the language and adapting it to recent biblical scholarship. It organizes the prose into paragraphs, indents the poetry, and occasionally notes in the margin any wording discrepancies among ancient manuscripts. It's scholarly and popular (an American version hits in 1901) and is widely considered the great-granddaddy of modern translations.

> "Odd, the way the less the Bible is read, the more it is translated."
> —C.S. Lewis
> (1898–1963)

Which brings us to today. At this moment in biblical history, there are dozens of scholarly translations of the Bible. And each of those new translations—the New International Version (NIV), the New King James Version (NKJV), the New American Standard Bible (NASB)—has spawned dozens of marketing-driven biblical packages. *The NIV Women's Devotional Bible. The Catholic Couples Bible. The Purpose-Driven Pimply Teen Boy's Extreme Study Bible.*[2] Recent years have even brought us a text-message-speak translation for your cell phone ("In da Bginnin God cre8d da heavens & da earth").

There are tons of Bible translations out there. Which one should you read?

## THREE TRANSLATING PHILOSOPHIES YOU NEED TO KNOW FIRST

*1. FORMAL EQUIVALENCE.* A Bible translation-related phrase that means translators try to follow the original document word for

---

1. Check out Young's version of John 3:16: "For God did so love the world, that His Son—the only begotten—He gave, that every one who is believing in him may not perish, but may have life age-during."

2. That last one's made up. Hopefully.

word, staying as close to the same grammatical order as appears in the original language. The resulting interpretation usually ends up harder to read but is more accurate—especially in retaining certain figures of speech or rhetorical patterns. The King James Version is an example.

**2. DYNAMIC EQUIVALENCE.** Instead of word-for-word interpretation, dynamic equivalence translations take a thought-for-thought approach. The goal is to reproduce, in English, the same *meaning* as the original—it wants the reader to understand the text in the same way the original Hebrew or Greek audience might have understood it.[3] The result is a less accurate translation in terms of word usage and grammar, but one that's easier to read and understand. The New International Version is an example.

**3. PARAPHRASE.** Speeds past thought-for-thought and careens to the next stop: meaning-for-meaning. Biblical paraphrases try to take the content and tone of the original language and convert it into contemporary English. (Sort of like chapters 4 and 5 of this book, but verse by verse. And much more scholarly.) These are really easy reading, but they give serious academics and paranoid fundies the hives. The Message, by Eugene Peterson, is a popular paraphrase. Now, on to the translations themselves ...

## THE KING JAMES VERSION/AUTHORIZED VERSION (KJV/AVI611)

**FIRST PUBLISHED IN:** 1611, by the Church of England, at King James' behest

**TRANSLATION STYLE:** Formal Equivalence

**QUICK DESCRIPTION:** The great-granddaddy of English Bibles and what you probably default to when reciting the Lord's Prayer or the Twenty-third Psalm or the Christmas Story from the

---

3. In fact, almost all translations from any language into another one use dynamic equivalence, to a certain degree.

book of Luke. Pretty much the most important book in Western civilization.

**WHY YOU SHOULD READ IT:** Because this is what the Bible's supposed to *sound* like, Jethro. All the rich, grandiose language—with verbs ending in *-eth* and a host of *thees* and *thous*—make it seem, well, holier than modern translations. Plus, if you don't read this version, you're apparently going to hell.[4]

**NOT SO FAST:** The Shakespearean language sounds cool but can be difficult to understand. People who find the Bible incomprehensible probably came to this conclusion upon reading the archaic King James. And in that case, they're right. Plus, biblical scholarship has grown a lot since the seventeenth century, so modern versions are slightly more accurate.

**★★★✦☆** The average customer rating, in early 2006, of The Holy Bible Containing the Old and New Testaments: King James Version, Black Imitation Leather (Hardcover) on Amazon.com.
(Based on 198 customer reviews.)

**EXAMPLES:**

*"Thou shalt not make unto thee any graven image, or any likeness of any thing that is in heaven above, or that is in the earth beneath, or that is in the water under the earth"* (Exod. 20:4).

*"For God so loved the world, that he gave his only begotten Son, that whosoever believeth in him should not perish, but have everlasting life"* (John 3:16).

## THE REVISED STANDARD VERSION (RSV)

**FIRST PUBLISHED IN:** 1952, by Thomas Nelson & Sons
**TRANSLATION STYLE:** Formal Equivalence

---

4. This is the viewpoint of a branch of extremely fundamentalist Independent Baptist Churches, who believe the 1611 Authorized Version of the Bible to be divinely inspired—in addition to, and occasionally in place of, the original manuscripts. Most of this line of thinking developed during the whole demon-RSV brouhaha. (For details, keep reading.)

**QUICK DESCRIPTION:** The first serious challenger to the King James, mainly a re-translation that builds on its solid base while trying to make the text more understandable. It keeps much of the familiar phraseology of the King James, including the *thees* and *thous* ... but only in reference to God.

**WHY YOU SHOULD READ IT:** Because it still feels like the King James but is a teensy bit more modern.

**NOT SO FAST:** Hardly anyone reads this version anymore, so you'll be all alone in your RSV devotion. Plus, some folks think this translation is tainted by godless liberalism. Why? Because the RSV's translation of Isaiah 7:14—a verse traditionally considered to be a prophecy of Christ's birth—replaces "virgin" with "young woman."[5] Incensed, some Christians take to burning this translation in the years immediately following its release. Before long, they're charging members of the translation panel with communism. Senator Joseph McCarthy even sticks his red-sniffing nose in the fray. Nice.

**EXAMPLES:**

*"You shall not make for yourself a graven image, or any likeness of anything that is in heaven above, or that is in the earth beneath, or that is in the water under the earth"* (Exod. 20:4).

*"For God so loved the world that he gave his only Son, that whoever believes in him should not perish but have eternal life"* (John 3:16).

# THE JERUSALEM BIBLE (JB)

**FIRST PUBLISHED IN:** 1966, by Darton Longman & Todd, Ltd. and Doubleday

**TRANSLATION STYLE:** Dynamic Equivalence

**QUICK DESCRIPTION:** The first English translation the pope

---

5. "Young woman" is actually the more accurate translation of the Hebrew word *almah*, which is used in the Isaiah passage and is not, in fact, a technical word for "virgin." *But* it generally appears in the context of virginity. And when the Gospel writer references the Isaiah phrase in Matthew 1:23, he uses "virgin" for sure. So, obviously, communism is involved.

allows to be made from the original languages, rather than the Latin Vulgate. It's initially published in French by a group of monks working in Jerusalem. (That's where the name comes from, and it's a good thing they weren't working in Toad Suck, Arkansas.) Based on its success, they get to work immediately on an English one.

**WHY YOU SHOULD READ IT:** It was the first widely accepted Catholic English translation of the Bible, and its impeccable scholarship and linguistic style win both Catholic and Protestant fans. As a bonus, one of the English stylists to work with the translators is none other than J.R.R. Tolkien, of *The Lord of the Rings* fame. Which means the Jerusalem Bible is preferred by four out of five fanboys.

**NOT SO FAST:** Its introductions and notes tend to lean leftward in terms of doctrine, so it makes conservative Bible readers a little itchy. Plus, there's that part where Gandalf shows up to help Joshua defeat the Gibeonites along the Beth Horon Pass.

### EXAMPLES:

*"You shall not make yourself a carved image or any likeness of anything in heaven or on earth beneath or in the waters under the earth"* (Exod. 20:4).

*"Yes, God loved the world so much that he gave his only Son, so that everyone who believes in him may not be lost but may have eternal life"* (John 3:16).

## THE NEW AMERICAN BIBLE (NAB)

**FIRST PUBLISHED IN:** 1970, by the Catholic Bible Association of America

**TRANSLATION STYLE:** Formal Equivalence

**QUICK DESCRIPTION:** The official Roman Catholic Bible for public reading and, along with the Jerusalem Bible, one of the

Catholic Church's most popular translations.

**WHY YOU SHOULD READ IT:** If you're a Catholic, this is what's being read at Mass. Plus, the high-quality translation maintains the delicate balance between word-for-word equivalence and good readin'.

**NOT SO FAST:** The footnotes are chock-a-block with Catholic doctrine, so Protestants may be a little uncomfortable with all the popishness and references to church councils. Plus, there's that whole Apocrypha section to worry about.

**EXAMPLES:**

*"You shall not carve idols for yourselves in the shape of anything in the sky above or on the earth below or in the waters beneath the earth"* (Exod. 20:4).

*"For God so loved the world that he gave his only Son, so that everyone who believes in him might not perish but might have eternal life"* (John 3:16).

> **According to the King James Version of Leviticus 11:29–30, these things are unclean to you: weasels, mice, tortoises, ferrets, chameleons, lizards, snails, and moles.**

# THE NEW AMERICAN STANDARD BIBLE (NASB)

**FIRST PUBLISHED IN:** 1971, by the Lockman Foundation

**TRANSLATION STYLE:** Mega-Formal Equivalence

**QUICK DESCRIPTION:** By far, the most literal of the modern translations. On the occasion that a strict word-for-word translation just doesn't make sense to contemporary ears, it footnotes the literal meaning.

**WHY YOU SHOULD READ IT:** It's faithful to the original language without succumbing to any theological leanings.

**NOT SO FAST:** The literalness of it makes for some confusing sentence constructions. The thing's accurate, but it's no page-turner. Plus, the original version prints verses as individual units instead of paragraphs, and that's annoying. Plus *plus*, it can easily be confused with the New American Bible—the Catholic version mentioned above, which includes the Apocrypha. That's a crisis of faith just waiting to happen.

> According to the New International Version of Leviticus 11:29–30, *these* things are unclean to you: weasels, rats, any kind of great lizard, geckos, monitor lizards, wall lizards, skinks, and chameleons. It's clear the translators of the NIV had some sort of crazy lizard-phobia.

**EXAMPLES:**

*"You shall not make for yourself an idol, or any likeness of what is in heaven above or on the earth beneath or in the water under the earth"* (Exod. 20:4).

*"For God so loved the world, that He gave His only begotten Son, that whoever believes in Him shall not perish, but have eternal life"* (John 3:16).

## THE LIVING BIBLE (TLB)

**FIRST PUBLISHED IN:** 1971, by Tyndale House Publishers

**TRANSLATION STYLE:** Paraphrase

**QUICK DESCRIPTION:** A bestseller in the early '70s, The Living Bible is a flat-out paraphrase by publisher and author Kenneth Taylor. The language is as clear and conversational as, well, a conversation.

**WHY YOU SHOULD READ IT:** It's as readable as any Bible gets. Taylor got the idea while trying to explain difficult passages to his children, so he wrote it with that audience in mind. In that regard, it works pretty well. Unless you're reading the really violent parts.

**NOT SO FAST:** It's a paraphrase of an English translation (according to Taylor, he paraphrased it from the 1901 American Standard Version), so it's not the most accurate Bible on the shelf when it comes to the original languages.

**EXAMPLES:**

*"You shall not make yourselves any idols: any images resembling animals, birds, or fish"* (Exod. 20:4).

*"For God loved the world so much that he gave his only Son so that anyone who believes in him shall not perish but have eternal life"* (John 3:16).

# THE NEW INTERNATIONAL VERSION (NIV)

**FIRST PUBLISHED IN:** 1978, by the International Bible Society and Zondervan Publishing House

**TRANSLATION STYLE:** Dynamic Equivalence

**QUICK DESCRIPTION:** The eight-hundred-pound gorilla of modern English translations. By far, the NIV has become the most popular translation in the world, having sold a staggering 150 million copies since being introduced. The translators are more interested in hitting the original meanings of certain words and phrases than maintaining word-for-word accuracy.[6]

**WHY YOU SHOULD READ IT:** Everyone else reads it. The NIV is big among American Evangelicals for its high readability and accuracy.

**NOT SO FAST:** You can't get the NIV with any of the deuterocanonical/apocryphal books in it—it's a Protestant-only translation. Plus, the NIV may be a perversion of Scripture made by translators under demonic influence (!) with the intent of denying the deity of Christ and, furthermore, pushing a homosexual agenda!

---

6. Here's an example. Mark 6:37 references "two hundred denarii" in the NASB. The NIV translates this "eight months of a man's wages," then footnotes the literal meaning.

No, really. Certain advocates of King James–only Bible reading actually believe this, so beware the NIV's corrupting influence.[7]

**EXAMPLES:**

*"You shall not make for yourself an idol in the form of anything in heaven above or on the earth beneath or in the waters below"* (Exod. 20:4).

*"For God so loved the world that he gave his one and only Son, that whoever believes in him shall not perish but have eternal life"* (John 3:16).

# THE NEW KING JAMES VERSION (NKJV)

**FIRST PUBLISHED IN:** 1982, by Thomas Nelson, Inc.

**TRANSLATION STYLE:** Formal Equivalence

**QUICK DESCRIPTION:** A brand-new translation made to keep the same phrasing and feel of the old King James. By keeping that pedigreed name on the cover, the publishers hope to attract any loyal KJV readers looking for something a little less stuffy. Or, in the case of the NIV haters, less demonic.

**WHY YOU SHOULD READ IT:** It's a good, solid, accurate translation with familiar phrasing and wordplay. It sticks closely to the original languages, which is why serious Bible scholars tend to like it.

**NOT SO FAST:** But because it's more concerned with accuracy than readability, it ends up jamming modern words into archaic sentence structure, which is kinda weird. Also, it translates from the same documents available to the original King James translators— notably Erasmus' *Textus Receptus*[8]—rather than earlier documents and texts (though it does indicate where some manuscripts differ).

**EXAMPLES:**

*"You shall not make for yourself a carved image—any likeness of anything that is in heaven above, or that is in the earth beneath, or that is in*

---

7. For a clear-thinking, evenhanded evaluation of the whole KJV-is-infallible-and-everything-else-is-of-the-devil controversy, read *The King James Only Controversy*, by James R. White (Grand Rapids: Bethany House, 1995).

8. Remember the *Textus Receptus*? It's the Greek text of the New Testament, published by Erasmus in the sixteenth century. For better or worse, it ends up being the primary source for the King James Version of the New Testament.

*the water under the earth"* (Exod. 20:4).

*"For God so loved the world that He gave His only begotten Son, that whoever believes in Him should not perish but have everlasting life"* (John 3:16).

## THE NEW JERUSALEM BIBLE (NJB)

**FIRST PUBLISHED IN:** 1985, by Darton Longman & Todd, Ltd. and Doubleday

**TRANSLATION STYLE:** Dynamic Equivalence

**QUICK DESCRIPTION:** An update to the Jerusalem Bible. Not quite as literary but slightly more literal. And with more inclusive language. Still pretty scholarly, still pretty eloquent.[9]

## THE NEW REVISED STANDARD VERSION (NRSV)

**FIRST PUBLISHED IN:** 1989, by the National Council of Churches

**TRANSLATION STYLE:** Formal Equivalence

> **Fanciful Creature Alert:**
> In the King James Version of Job 39:9, Yahweh asks a rhetorical question about unicorns. In modern translations, the word *unicorn* is replaced by "wild ox."

**QUICK DESCRIPTION:** Just like the RSV, only it gets rid of the old-fashioned language. It's *thee*-free. Also, it uses gender-inclusive language: "brothers" becomes "brothers and sisters." Controversy!

## THE NEW LIVING TRANSLATION

**FIRST PUBLISHED IN:** 1996, by Tyndale House Publishers

**TRANSLATION STYLE:** Dynamic Equivalence

**QUICK DESCRIPTION:** A revision of The Living Bible to

9. The *Pocket Guide* is forgoing the biblical examples for this "new" revision to the Jerusalem Bible—as well as for other "new" versions, including the NRSV, ESV, and TNIV—since these contain only slight language updates. The grammar and syntax hardly change enough to burden you with samples.

increase its accuracy while maintaining readability. Based on current biblical scholarship and produced by an interdenominational team of ninety scholars, the result is a solid, thought-for-thought translation. Not quite as readable as the original, but close.

Fanciful Creature Alert #2: Satyrs (half-men/half-goats from Greek mythology) get shoutouts in the King James Version in Isaiah 13:21. Modern versions translate this as "wild goats."

*EXAMPLES:*

*"Do not make idols of any kind, whether in the shape of birds or animals or fish"* (Exod. 20:4).

*"For God so loved the world that he gave his only Son, so that everyone who believes in him will not perish but have eternal life"* (John 3:16).

## THE ENGLISH STANDARD VERSION (ESV)

**FIRST PUBLISHED IN:** 2001, by Crossway Books

**TRANSLATION STYLE:** Formal Equivalence

**QUICK DESCRIPTION:** Another gentle update of the RSV, but without the controversial gender-inclusive stuff in the NRSV. Or the communism.

## THE MESSAGE (MSG)

**COMPLETE VERSION FIRST PUBLISHED IN:** 2002, by NavPress

**TRANSLATION STYLE:** Paraphrase

**QUICK DESCRIPTION:** A contemporary paraphrase from the original languages by Eugene H. Peterson, a prolific pastor, scholar, and author with impeccable credentials in the evangelical world. It's originally written to recapture the informal "street language" of the New Testament, resulting in a rhythm and flavor completely different from any other Bible translation.

**WHY YOU SHOULD READ IT:** It's in common, readable English but doesn't sound at all like a children's Bible. Plus, you get occasional fun idiomatic expressions like this: "They traded the glory of God … for cheap figurines you can buy at any roadside stand" (Rom. 1:23).

**NOT SO FAST:** Some think The Message is an appalling distortion of God's Word, riddled with deletions, alterations, and additions to the original text. Then again, most of these same naysayers also believe the NIV to be personally endorsed by Satan.

**EXAMPLES:**

*"No carved gods of any size, shape, or form of anything whatever, whether of things that fly or walk or swim"* (Exod. 20:4).

*"This is how much God loved the world: He gave his Son, his one and only Son. And this is why: so that no one need be destroyed; by believing in him, anyone can have a whole and lasting life"* (John 3:16).

# TODAY'S NEW INTERNATIONAL VERSION (TNIV)

**FIRST PUBLISHED IN:** 2005, by International Bible Society and Zondervan Publishing House

**TRANSLATION STYLE:** Dynamic Equivalence

**QUICK DESCRIPTION:** A controversial revision of the NIV that uses gender-neutral language (much like the NRSV). So phrases like "sons of God" become "children of God." And any general reference to "a man" changes to "a person." Which is cool until the three Wise Persons show up to deliver gifts to the baby Jesus. (Kidding.) Anyway, there's a big to-do about the whole thing, and several prominent evangelical persons are not fans of this translation.

# A FEW OTHER, LESS-POPULAR VERSIONS YOU MAY ENCOUNTER

The New English Bible (1970), Today's English Version/Good News Bible (1976),[10] Revised English Bible (1989), Contemporary English Version (1991), and the Southern Baptist–approved Holman Christian Standard Bible (2004).

All of these are dynamic equivalence translations, in case you were wondering.

---

10. The New Testament version of this translation was first published under the title *Good News for Modern Man* in 1966, complete with stick-figure illustrations. It sold more than thirty million copies over the next five years. Good news, indeed.

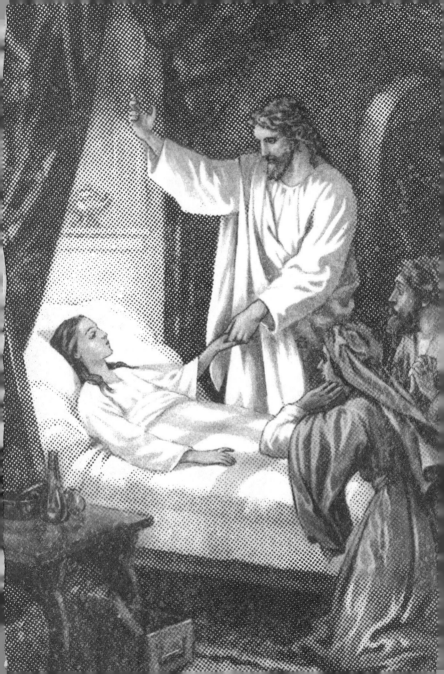

# LIST YE BE SMITTEN
## (BIBLICAL FLOTSAM AND JETSAM)

he *Pocket Guide* draws to a close with this brief collection of Bible-related lists, arranged in no particular order and containing little of any particular importance. Don't let that keep you from a pleasurable reading experience, though. What follows is a scriptural medley of names, rules, deaths, activities, and statements with tenuous connections to anything else in this book. Enjoy.

## FIVE HEALTH CONDITIONS THAT SOUND ABSOLUTELY AWFUL, AS DESCRIBED IN THE KING JAMES

**1)** *Dry scall* (Lev. 13:30). What it is: leprosy
**2)** *Grievous murrain* (Exod. 9:3). What it is: livestock plague

**3)** *The burning ague* (Lev. 26:16). What it is: fever

**4)** *Smited bowels* (2 Chron. 21:18). What it is: a serious bowel disease

**5)** *Bloody flux* (Acts 28:8). What it is: dysentery

# THE FOUR BEST MOMENTS FOR DONKEYS

**1** *Balaam's donkey speaks* (Num. 22:23–30). In one of the most original biblical miracles ever, Balaam's donkey is given the gift of speech when his master encounters an angel of the Lord on the path. Even weirder, Balaam jumps right in and engages the suddenly literate beast of burden in conversation, without so much as batting an eyelash.

**2** *Samson kills a thousand Philistines with the "jawbone of an ass"* (Judg. 15:13–17). And while today, Jackie Chan-types can turn pool cues and potted plants into deadly armaments, the donkey-bone-as-weapon trend never really catches on.

**3** *Donkeys praised for their large genitals* (Ezek. 23:20). No, really. And by none other than God himself, in a sexually explicit metaphor condemning Israel's unfaithfulness.

**4** *Jesus makes his triumphal entry on the back of a donkey* (Mark 11:1–11). Which cements the humble donkey as one of the earth's holiest creatures. Or, perhaps, not.

# NINE MISCELLANEOUS THINGS YOU MUST NOT DO, ACCORDING TO THE LAW OF MOSES

1) **Boil** a young goat in its mother's milk (Exod. 23:19).
2) **Eat** a bat (Lev. 11:19).
3) **Audibly mock** the deaf, or attempt to trip the blind (Lev. 19:14).
4) **Wear** a garment that mixes linen and wool (Lev. 19:19).
5) **Disfigure** the edges of your beard (Lev. 19:27).
6) **Cut down** the trees of a city while you are besieging it (Deut. 20:19).
7) **Hide and refuse to help** upon seeing your brother's donkey or ox fall down in the road (Deut. 22:4).
8) **Charge** interest on a loan, unless it's a loan to a foreigner (Deut. 23:19–20).
9) **Pity** a woman who gets her hand cut off because she grabbed the genitals of a man who was attacking her husband (Deut. 25:11–12).

## SEVEN BIBLICAL SUICIDES

**1** *Abimelech* (Judg. 9:50–54). One of Gideon's sons and the ruler of Shechem, who gets a millstone dropped on his melon during a battle at Thebez. Because a woman did the rock-dropping—and because Abimelech can't stand the thought of having been gravely injured by a stinkin' girl—he commands his armor-bearer to kill him.

**2** *Samson* (Judg. 16:26–30). The OT's shaggy-haired, sightless Superman who pulls down the pillars of a great Philistine temple, squashing his captors and, in the process, himself.

**3** *Israel's King Saul* (1 Sam. 31:1–4). Impales himself on his own sword, after being poked through with arrows during a devastating loss to the Philistines. Afraid he might be "abused" by "uncircumcised men," he ask his armor-bearer to do the dirty work. The servant refuses, so Saul's gotta do it himself. If there ever wasn't a time for insubordination ...

**4** *King Saul's Armor-Bearer* (1 Sam. 31:5). Apparently, once his boss has Cobained himself, the armor-bearer has nothing to live for. So he, too, comes to a self-inflicted pointy end.

**5** *Ahithophel* (2 Sam. 17:23). One of David's wise counselors who sides with Absalom in his revolt against David. Wise, indeed, but very sensitive. When Absalom ignores his advice, Ahithophel hangs himself.

**6** *Israel's King Zimri* (1 Kings 16:18). After killing a drunk King Elah and parking his own butt on the throne, he gets attacked by Omri, commander of Elah's army. When Omri takes the royal city, Zimri burns his newly acquired house down ... but forgets to leave before flicking his Bic.

**7** *Judas Iscariot.* Betrays Jesus, feels bad about it—imagine that—and goes out and hangs himself (Matt. 27:5). Either that, or he buys a field, falls down in it, and spills his guts out (Acts 1:18). We're not sure which.

## TEN USES OF THE NUMBER 'FORTY'

**1)** *Noah's flood* (Gen. 7:4). It rains for forty days and nights.

**2)** *The Mountain of the Lord* (Exod. 24:18). Moses hangs out on Mount Sinai for forty days and nights prior to receiving the Ten Commandments.

**3)** *Spying on milk and honey* (Num. 13:25). Moses' spies poke around Canaan for forty days.

**4)** *Lost* (Num. 14:34). The people of Israel wander around in the desert for forty years before reaching the Promised Land.

**5)** *Giant smackathon* (1 Sam. 17:16). Goliath teases Israel for forty days before David rocks his world.

**6)** *David's reign* (1 Kings 2:11). King David rules Israel for forty years.

**7)** *Solomon's reign* (1 Kings 11:42). David's son, Solomon, also rules Israel for forty years.

**8)** *God's ultimatum* (Jon. 3:4). Jonah tells the people of Ninevah they've got forty days to shape up.

**9)** *Jesus gets hungry* (Matt. 4:2). Prior to being tempted, Jesus fasts in the wilderness for forty days.

**10)** *Jesus' second act* (Acts 1:3). Forty days pass between the resurrection and ascension of Jesus.

## ONE STATEMENT BY PAUL THAT, WHEN TAKEN OUT OF CONTEXT, MAKES HIM SOUND RELATIVELY HIP

"Peace to the brothers" (Eph. 6:23).

**177**

## TWENTY-SIX OF DAVID'S MIGHTY MEN WHOSE NAMES MYSTIFY SPELLCHECK[1]

| | |
|---|---|
| Abi–Albon | Helez |
| Abiezer | Hezro |
| Ahiam | Hiddai |
| Asahel | Igal |
| Azmaveth | Ithai |
| Benaiah | Maharai |
| Elhanan | Mebunnai |
| Eliahba | Naharai |
| Eliam | Paarai |
| Elika | Shammah |
| Eliphelet | Uriah |
| Gareb | Zalmon |
| Heled | Zelek |

## TWO MIGHTY MEN THAT SPELLCHECK LIKES

Ira

Jonathan

## NINE PEOPLE GOD SMITES

**1** *Lot's wife* (Gen. 19:26). For looking back at the destruction of Sodom. God turns her into a pillar of salt.

**2** *Onan* (Gen. 38:8–10). For spilling his semen onto the ground instead of depositing it in the womb of his brother's wife.

1. As listed in 2 Samuel 23:24–39.

**3** & **4** *Nadab and Abihu* (Lev. 10:1–2). For offering "unauthorized fire" before the Lord as priests.

**5** *Korah* (Num. 16:30–32). Swallowed up by a big hole in the ground for trying to overthrow Moses.

**6** *Nabal* (1 Sam. 25:38). For being an arrogant drunk and general annoyance to David.

**7** *Uzzah* (2 Sam. 6:6–7). For unceremoniously steadying the Ark of the Covenant when it starts to fall.

**8** & **9** *Ananias and Sapphira* (Acts 5:1–10). For lying to the Holy Spirit, and Peter, about a real estate transaction.

## THREE BIBLICAL EXCUSES ONE MIGHT STILL APPROPRIATE IN CERTAIN SITUATIONS

1) *"I'm a bad public speaker"* (Exod. 4:10). Moses, on why he's not the ideal choice for leading the Israelites out of Egypt.
2) *"Those people made me do it"* (Exod. 32:22–24). Aaron, on why he melted down a bunch of jewelry to make the Israelites a worshipable golden calf while Moses was hanging with God on Mount Sinai.
3) *"This isn't the best time"* (Acts 24:25). Felix, the governor of Judea, postponing a response after Paul delivers the Gospel message to him.

## FOUR BIBLICAL EXCUSES THAT NO LONGER WORK VERY WELL

**1)** *"A talking serpent deceived me"* (Gen. 3:13). Eve, when God questions her and Adam about eating from the forbidden tree.

**2)** *"I might be overtaken by evil in the mountains"* (Gen. 19:19). Lot, trying to think of a good reason to stay in the doomed, decadent Sodom.

**3)** *"Giants"* (Num. 13:31–33). Ten of the Israelite spies, explaining why the thought of fighting their way into the Promised Land gives them the shivers.

**4)** *"I just bought five yoke of oxen and need to test them"* (Luke 14:19). A character in the parable of the great supper, on why he can't make it to a wedding feast.

## SEVEN NON-CANONICAL BOOKS MENTIONED BY NAME IN THE OLD TESTAMENT

**1)** The Book of Wars (Num. 21:14)

**2)** The Book of Jashar (Josh. 10:13)

**3)** The Book of the Annals of King David (1 Chron. 27:24)

**4)** The Records of Nathan the Prophet (1 Chron. 29:29)

**5)** The Records of Gad the Seer (1 Chron. 29:29)

**6)** The Annotations of the Prophet Iddo (2 Chron. 13:22)

**7)** The Annals of Jehu, Son of Hanani (2 Chron. 20:34)

## SIX BIBLICAL MAGICIANS, WITCHES, SORCERORS, AND/OR FORTUNETELLERS

**①** & **②** *Jannes and Jambres* (Exod. 7:11). The magicians of Pharaoh's court, who turn walking sticks into snakes in imitation of Moses and Aaron's trickery.[2]

**③** *The Witch of Endor* (1 Sam. 28). A medium consulted by King Saul to orchestrate a séance so he can have a discussion with the dead prophet Samuel. She pulls it off, and Saul freaks out.

**④** *Simon the Sorceror* (Acts 8:9–24). A magician in Samaria who tries to buy the power of the Holy Spirit from Peter and John. Because, oh, the tricks he could do!

**⑤** *Elymas the Sorceror* (Acts 13:6–11). A false prophet in Cyprus who tries to keep the island's proconsul from hearing about God from Paul and Barnabas.

**⑥** *The Philippian Fortuneteller* (Acts 16:16–18). A demon-possessed, future-predicting slave girl in Philippi, whose evil spirit is cast out by Paul. This irritates her owners, because the girl's mad soothsaying skills are, well, demon-spawned.

2. Jannes and Jambres are introduced in Exodus 7, but we don't learn their names until 2 Timothy 3:8.

## TWELVE BIBLICAL NAMES THAT ARE STILL POPULAR TODAY

1) Rachel
2) David
3) Michael
4) Ruth
5) Joshua
6) Mary
7) John
8) Luke
9) Jacob
10) James
11) Daniel
12) Martha

## TWELVE BIBLICAL NAMES THAT ARE CONSIDERABLY LESS POPULAR TODAY

1) Ham (Gen. 5:32)
2) Nimrod (Gen. 10:8)
3) Zipporah (Exod. 2:21)
4) Hobab (Num. 10:29)
5) Agag (Num. 24:7)
6) Shishak (1 Kings 11:40)
7) Evil-Merodach (2 Kings 25:27)
8) Mephibosheth (2 Sam. 4:4)
9) Quirinius (Luke 2:2)
10) Dorcas (Acts 9:36)
11) Crispus (Acts 18:8)
12) Gaius (Acts 19:29)

## FOUR ACTIVITIES OF MICHAEL THE ARCHANGEL

1 **Breaks** through some sort of spiritual gridlock on behalf of a fellow angel who's detained by the twenty-one-day stalling tactic of the "prince of the Persian kingdom" (Dan. 10:13). And, no, the *Pocket Guide* has no idea what this passage means either.

2 **Protects** the people of God during "a time of distress"—which some interpret to be the Great Tribulation (Dan. 12:1).

**3** **Argues** with the devil about the body of Moses, but politely declines to slander him (Jude 1:9).

**4** **Throws** down with the dragon at the end of the world (Rev. 12:7).

## ONE PHRASE FROM THE KING JAMES VERSION, USED GENERICALLY TO DESCRIBE MALES, THAT RAISES EYEBROWS WHEN EMPLOYED IN GENERAL CONVERSATION

"Any who pisseth against the wall" (1 Sam. 25:22, 34; 1 Kings 14:10, 16:11, 21:21; 2 Kings 9:8).

## NINE OFFENSES THAT, UNDER LEVITICAL LAW, COULD GET YOU EXECUTED

**1)** Being a witch, medium, or sorceress (Exod. 22:18).

**2)** Cursing your father or mother (Lev. 20:9).

**3)** Committing adultery (Lev. 20:10).

**4)** Practicing homosexuality (Lev. 20:13).

**5)** Simultaneously being married to both a woman and her mother (Lev. 20:14).

**6)** Mating with an animal (Lev. 20:15–16).

**7)** Gathering sticks on the Sabbath (Num. 15:32–36).

**8)** Being a rebellious son (Deut. 21:18–21).

**9)** As a woman, not showing sufficient evidence of your virginity on your wedding night (Deut. 22:20–21).

## SEVEN LESSER-KNOWN BIBLE STORIES THAT PROBABLY SHOULDN'T BE TOLD TO CHILDREN

**1** *Lot and the Men of Sodom* (Gen. 19:1–11), in which an angry mob tries to break down Lot's door so they can get it on with Lot's two angelic visitors. Out of loyalty to his guests, Lot refuses, and offers his two virgin daughters instead. Ah ... family values.

**2** *Abimelech Slaughters His Family* (Judg. 9:1–6), in which Abimelech, the son of Gideon, wants to become king and thus murders seventy of his brothers to eliminate the competition.

**3** *The Gibeah Outrage* (Judg. 19), in which a man and his concubine spend the night at the home of an old guy near Gibeah. A bunch of locals show up and—in a scene reminiscent of Sodom—demand the old guy shove his guest out the door so they can rape him. The homeowner refuses and instead hands over the concubine. The crowd gang-rapes her. The next morning, the man finds her in a bloody heap outside the door. She's dead, or close to it. So he hauls her inside, cuts her into twelve pieces, and dispatches a piece to each of the twelve tribes scattered across Israel.

**4** *David's Engagement Gift* (1 Sam. 18:17–29), in which David and his men slaughter two hundred Philistines so David can collect their foreskins as a present for Saul. In exchange, David gets to marry Saul's daughter, Michal. Sometimes the most romantic gifts are those least expected.

**5** *The Rape of Tamar* (2 Sam. 13), in which Tamar, the beautiful daughter of David and sister of Absalom, is raped by her half-brother

Amnon. Absalom gets revenge two years later by having his servants get Amnon good and drunk. Then they kill him.

**6** *The Reign of King Menahem* (2 Kings 15:16), in which Menahem assumes the throne of Israel after killing King Shallum, and then goes on a rampage against his neighboring foes. During which he locates all the enemies' pregnant women and rips open their wombs.

**7** *King Ahaz's Worship Practices* (2 Chron. 28:1–4), in which Ahaz gets involved in the worship of false gods, to whom he sacrifices his own children as burnt offerings.


# NINE BOOKS THAT CATHOLICS ACCEPT AS BIBLICAL, BUT PROTESTANTS DON'T[3]

**1)** Tobit
**2)** Judith
**3)** Esther (the Greek version)
**4)** Wisdom of Solomon
**5)** Sirach
**6)** Baruch (including the Letter of Jeremiah)
**7)** Extra stuff in the Book of Daniel (including the Song of the Three Young Men, Susanna, and Bel and the Dragon)
**8)** 1 Maccabees
**9)** 2 Maccabees


3. Catholics refer to these books as "deuterocanonical," meaning their canonical status was settled later than the earlier "protocanonical" books of the Bible, which were adopted into the Hebrew canon by Jewish leadership in the first century. Instead, they show up in the Septuagint Greek text of the Old Testament. Protestants usually call these books "the Apocrypha." Or "those weird Catholic books."

## SEVEN PHRASES FROM THE BOOK OF JUDGES THAT WOULD MAKE AWESOME BAND NAMES

**1)** The Nether Springs (1:15, KJV)
**2)** Cushan-Rishathaim (3:8)
**3)** The Heads of Oreb and Zeeb (7:25)
**4)** Millo (9:6)
**5)** Forsake My Sweetness (9:11, KJV)
**6)** The Tribe of Dan (18:30)
**7)** Certain Sons of Belial (19:22, KJV)

## TEN COMMON ENGLISH PHRASES WITH BIBLICAL ORIGINS

**1** *Forbidden fruit.* From Genesis 3, in which Adam and Eve snack on the fruit of the tree of the knowledge of good and evil, with disastrous results. God tosses them out of the Garden of Eden. (*Current meaning: anything that's tempting but dangerous.*)

**2** *Eye for an eye.* From Exodus 21:24, in reference to the Old Testament standard of justice that allows exact vengeance (and nothing more). So if a guy cuts off your arm, you're only allowed to cut off his arm. As opposed to *both* of his arms. Fair's fair. (*Current meaning: a demand for payback.*)

**3** *Scapegoat.* From a symbolic event on the Day of Atonement, when the high priest would lay his hands on a goat, confess Israel's sins upon it, then send the animal off into the wilderness to "carry away" the nation's sin. From Leviticus 16. (*Current meaning: anyone who gets blamed for someone else's mistake.*)

**4** *Can a leopard change its spots?* From a proverb found in Jeremiah 13:23. The leopard line comes right after a related but less-popular question: Can the Ethiopian change his skin? (*Current meaning: you can't change who you are, except via plastic surgery.*)

**5** *Going the extra mile.* From the Sermon on the Mount in Matthew 5. Back in the day, the ruling Romans could command a Jew to carry something for them for up to a mile. Jesus tells his followers to do more than what's required of them. How? By carrying the stuff a second mile, out of love. (*Current meaning: to do more than is asked or expected.*)

**6** *Turn the other cheek.* Also from the Sermon on the Mount in Matthew 5. Instead of the old "eye for an eye" system, Jesus says not to resist an evil person when he slaps your cheek. Let him take a shot at the other cheek, too. (*Current meaning: to take abuse without complaining or retaliating.*)

**7** *Physician, heal thyself.* From a proverb Jesus quotes in Luke 4:23, to explain why no prophet is ever accepted in his hometown. (*Current meaning: quit pointing out my faults and fix your own.*)

**8** *Good Samaritan.* From Jesus' parable in Luke 10, about a Samaritan guy who stops at the side of the road to take care of a Jew—his enemy—who's been beaten up and left for dead. (*Current meaning: anyone who goes out of his or her way to help a stranger.*)

**9** *Kill the fatted calf.* From Luke 15:23 (KJV), in the parable of the prodigal son. When the sinful son returns home after blowing his inheritance on hookers and "wild living," his father celebrates by ordering up a family barbecue. (*Current meaning: to celebrate with a major party.*)

**⑩** *It's better to give than receive.* From Paul's goodbye speech to the leaders of the church in Ephesus, recorded in Acts 20:35. He's actually quoting Jesus ... only the statement doesn't appear anywhere in the Gospels. (*Current meaning: it's better to give than, um, receive.*)

# SELECTED BIBLIOGRAPHY

The following titles were invaluable resources in the writing of this book, and they're much more scholarly than the *Pocket Guide*. So, clearly, any mistakes in this book are the responsibility of the authors below. (Kidding. The *Pocket Guide* accepts full blame for any unbridled ignorance.)

Michael D. Coogan, Ed., *The Oxford History of the Biblical World* (New York: Oxford University Press, 1998).

F.L. Cross, Ed., and F.L. Cross and E.A. Livingstone, Second Edition Eds., *The Oxford Dictionary of the Christian Church* (New York: Oxford University Press, 1983).

Christopher De Hamel, *The Book: A History of the Bible* (London: Phaidon Press, 2001).

Michael Gantt, *A NonChurchgoer's Guide to the Bible* (Intercourse, PA: Good Books, 1995).

Alister McGrath, *In the Beginning: The Story of the King James Bible and How It Changed a Nation, a Language, and a Culture* (New York: Doubleday, 2001).

Bruce M. Metzger & Michael D. Coogan, Eds., *The Oxford Companion to the Bible* (New York: Oxford University Press, 1993).

Allen C. Myers, Ed., and John W. Simpson Jr., Philip A. Frank, Timothy P. Jenney, and Ralph W. Vunderink, Associate Eds., *The Eerdmans Bible Dictionary* (Grand Rapids, MI: William B. Eerdmans Publishing Company, 1987).

Adam Nicolson, *God's Secretaries: The Making of the King James Bible* (New York: HarperCollins, 2003).

Stephen Ozment, *The Age of Reform, 1250–1550: An Intellectual and Religious History of Late Medieval and Reformation Europe* (New Haven, CT: Yale University Press, 1980).

Jaroslav Pelikan, *Whose Bible Is It? A History of the Scriptures Through the Ages* (New York: Viking, 2005).

Leland Ryken, Philip Ryken, and James Wilhoit, Eds., *Ryken's Bible Handbook: A Guide to Reading and Studying the Bible* (Carol Stream, IL: Tyndale House Publishers, 2005).

H.L. Willmington, *Willimington's Book of Bible Lists: More Than 6,000 Fascinating Items* (Wheaton, IL: Tyndale House Publishers, 1987).

Perhaps the best overall resource in the creation of this book was the indispensable online Bible at *www.biblegateway.com*. God bless the good folks at Gospel Communications International for providing a fully searchable eBible in dozens of languages and translations. Though the *Pocket Guide* rarely needed to compare, for instance, a passage from the 1934 Vietnamese Bible with the same passage in the Arabic Life Application Bible, it was nice just knowing it could be done. Thanks, Bible Gateway.

IF YOU LIKED THIS BOOK,
CHECK OUT THESE OTHER BOOKS
IN THE POCKET GUIDE SERIES:

## [RELEVANTBOOKS]

FOR MORE INFORMATION
ABOUT OTHER RELEVANT BOOKS,
check out www.relevantbooks.com.